Dr. LaHaye,

Thank you for your influence on our country and my life.

Pat Chappell

Rom 1:16

GUIDED BY GRACE
Servant Leadership for
the Local Church

GUIDED BY GRACE

Servant Leadership for the Local Church

By Dr. Paul Chappell

P. O. Box 1099, Murfreesboro, TN 37133

All Scripture quotations in this book are
taken from the King James Version.

Printed and Bound in the United States of America

To my best friend, counselor and wife, Terrie

Contents

SECTION 1
Identifying Spiritual Leadership

SECTION 2
21st-Century Leadership Challenges

SECTION 3
Establishing Leadership Requirements

SECTION 4
A Vision for Spiritual Leadership

SECTION 5
Making a Difference

SECTION 6
Final Challenge

Preface

Serving the Lord in Southern California has always been exciting! The trends of the culture, the beauty of the coast, the pace of living and the masses of people combine to create an adventurous backdrop to ministry.

Sometimes we get a little more excitement than we anticipated. Take last night, for instance, when an earthquake (7.2 magnitude) awakened our family. After we checked on the kids and checked the house, I turned to the news for more information. As usual, the news teams were out in full force "looking for a story." After hours of searching, it was discovered that the epicenter of the quake was in the middle of the Mojave Desert and that the only damage to report was an Amtrak train that had derailed.

As I observed the television picture of a train "off its track," I thought of the fate of many pastors and churches today. It appears to me that as we minister in these last days, Satan is doing all he can to derail the church from her mission. Only those leaders guided by God's grace will sustain the jolts of ministry.

Sometimes our leadership journey can seem like a long and "jerky" ride across the desert. Dry and desolate seasons face every servant of God. Because of this, we need to experience the reassuring grace of God's Spirit who will inspire, instruct and guide us on the next leg of the journey.

In order to pass through the desert and on to higher ground for God, you may need to assess your philosophy of leadership. Perhaps God will use trials or criticism to lead you to a place of spiritual renewal. Or you may need a fresh vision for your future ministry as a leader. The desert is a good place to find God's direction (just like Moses).

After God works in the hearts of His servant leaders, He equips them with a vision and enables them to face the challenges of spiritual oversight and the building of teams. Wherever you are in your development as a spiritual leader, it is my prayer that God will use *Guided by Grace* to encourage you to enjoy the journey as much as the destination. If the Adversary has been a source of derailment, then I pray also that the truths on these pages will remind you of your victory in Jesus and challenge you to stay on course for His glory.

Acknowledgments

As I read through the final proof of this book, I was reminded once again of the power of God to guide and shape our lives by His grace. I am also mindful that He often uses His people to help us assess and grow in the work unto which He has called us. I would like to thank Dr. David Gibbs for his friendship and counsel in my life. I would like to thank Dr. Don Sisk for his faithfulness to be an encourager and prayer warrior. Special thanks to my secretary, Bonnie Ferrso, for the countless hours of help she gave; to my editor, Melissa Baccarella, for her determination and creativity throughout the writing process; and to the staff at the Sword of the Lord for the great job in editing. Many thanks are also due to the faithful members of Lancaster Baptist Church who encourage their pastor to follow God's leading. Finally, praise to our Lord who saves, keeps, guides and leads us *by His grace.*

Section 1

Identifying Spiritual Leadership

CHAPTER 1

Enlisted in the Service of Grace

Not to the strong is the battle;
Not to the swift is the race;
Yet to the true and the faithful
Victory is promised through grace.
—Fanny Crosby[1]

Be all that you can be in the _____. Go ahead. Fill in the blank. This familiar army slogan is a call to service for our nation's youth. Recently I heard another army advertisement that boasts, **"We build leaders from the ground up."** While this may be a catchy phrase that reflects the humanistic philosophies permeating our culture, it also opposes the Biblical model of servant leadership. God is interested in building leaders **from Heaven down.** He disdains our feeble efforts to be all we can be (which isn't much); rather, He prefers that we become all that Christ is.

Good spiritual leaders are shepherds, not saviours; leaders, not lords; guides, not gods. When the tactics of men tend to political maneuvering, position may be gained, but it is without purpose. Human effort alone is a departure from the principle of grace in leadership. As spiritual leaders, our goal is Christ, not a particular pulpit, perks or position. So let us enlist in the service of grace where attitudes and ambitions are trained to reflect the mind of Christ.

Adversely, many of the leadership principles exercised in ministry today are borrowed from secular platforms and conveniently renamed. It is imperative that leaders embrace the Word of God as the only authoritative textbook for Christian leadership. It is from the Bible, which is "profitable for doctrine, for reproof, for correction, [and] for instruction in righteousness,"[2] that our standard operating procedures are derived.

Preparation for service always involves growth in the discipline of grace, which can be defined as a disposition created by the Holy Spirit of God in the life of a believer. Servant leaders are lifetime disciples—lifetime learners. By the grace of God, they **LEARN** to lead with a godly disposition that is created by the Holy Spirit. In his classic work, *Spiritual Leadership,* J. Oswald Sanders contrasts spiritual and fleshly leadership attributes:

Fleshly	*Spiritual*
Self-confident	Confident in God
Knows men	Also knows God
Makes own decisions	Seeks God's will
Ambitious	Humble
Creates methods	Follows God's example
Enjoys command	Delights in obedience to God
Seeks personal reward	Loves God and others
Independent	Depends on God[3]

Godly leading is possible because of the inner working of the Holy Spirit. This work of grace causes us to initiate ministry where we already see God at work and to wait when there are no orders from God. It enables us to forgive and to love when, as earthly leaders, we are inclined to harbor resentment. Each of us demonstrates a proclivity for building our ministries from the ground up (our way) rather than seeking the heart of God in every situation. In fact, most can recall instances of leadership failure that, if explored, could be tracked to a lack of growth in grace. The good news is that we serve a God who is the Author of second chances.

Because grace is the inner working and development of the Holy Spirit, only those who have been born again by the Spirit of God can attain the privilege of SERVING as a leader. This service begins with worship, and ministry to others is merely an extension of our worship of Him. Growth in the discipline of God's grace is the rock upon which spiritual leaders build their ministries. When growth in God's grace is absent from our lives, it is impossible to exhibit His love before a world that is weary of power politics and fleshly leadership.

The Scriptures charge us that, in addition to growing in grace, we should become **established** in it. We are admonished to avoid being "carried about with divers and strange doctrines. For it is a good thing that the heart be **established** with grace; not with meats, which have not profited them that have been occupied therein."[4]

The established life of grace rejoices in times of sorrow, forgives in the company of deceit and presses forward when reminded of past failures. How is this possible? It is a fact that the Spirit of grace develops the fruits of grace in the life of the servant who leads by grace.

Donald G. Barnhouse asserts that these fruits of grace partner to produce one fruit: love. It does not matter if we have "the gift of prophecy, and understand all mysteries, and all knowledge;...[and exercise] all faith, so...[we] could remove mountains"[5]—if we do not love, we are nothing. Mr. Barnhouse clarifies his point in the following way:

> **Joy** is love singing,
> **Peace** is love resting,
> **Long-suffering** is love enduring,
> **Gentleness** is love's true touch,
> **Goodness** is love's character,

Faith is love's habit,
Meekness is love's self-forgetfulness, and
Temperance is love holding the reins.[6]

These are the gifts and their manifestations that the Spirit of grace develops in the servant of grace.

A spiritual leader realizes that he can go only so far and for so long apart from God's grace before his life and ministry will be negatively affected by his neglect of the Holy Spirit. A leader will know if he has ceased to grow in grace only by way of self-examination. Onlookers will eventually notice the lack of grace, but wise is the leader who continues learning to hear that still small voice of God and obeys His every impulse. Two Biblical principles serve to gauge whether our ministry is being established in grace: the principles of focus and sight.

The first principle is that a spiritual leader's heart is utterly devoted to or *focused* upon God. Such undivided devotion does not leave room for common idolatries. Such immoderate attachments are reflected both in life and leadership. Therefore, a spiritual leader daily asks God to search his heart knowing that self-examination is complete when the measuring stick is God's Word and the initiator is His Spirit.

Idolatry is the dedication of our love, affection and allegiance to any person, object, pursuit or pleasure in place of, apart from or above our love and loyalty to God. A spouse or child, a job or ministry, a habit or hobby, material possessions or monetary wealth and financial security can become the personal and private idols to which we bow when no one is looking. These are not inherently sinful, but when allotted undue priority in our lives, they eclipse the power of the Spirit in our lives. This would be a good time to reflect that any believer who does not hate his father, mother, wife, children and other believers, as well as his own life, in comparison to his love for and focus upon Christ, is not a true disciple.[7]

The disciples were known to say to the Lord, "This is a hard saying." However, we can only fulfill our duties and privileges as husbands, fathers and pastors by loving God above all others. But can we love God more than we love ourselves? That is the hard part of the call to discipleship. How can one hate his own life? The most pervasive idol facing each of us is the one within us. The god of self ambushes our good intentions and prompts us to place the esteem of others before the esteem of God in an open demonstration of the "our way" attitude. Balance is the key.

For example, Jesus grew in favor with God and man. He exercised His human will in constant submission to the divine will. We may think, *Yes, well, that's Jesus.* However, we must acknowledge that we who are spiritually alive in Christ have the ability to exercise our human will in constant submission to God through the Spirit of the living God who indwells and empowers us. **The answer is submission.** At its root, idolatry is the opposite of submission. It divides the allegiance of the heart and distracts the focus of our spirit. A heart of grace contradicts that pattern because it is a pure heart, a submitted heart from which a life of service flows that is distinctively different and Christlike.

Jesus instructed His followers, saying, "Blessed are the pure in heart: for they shall see God."[8] **The second principle is spiritual *sight* or discernment, which is born of our desire to see God at work.** While human effort has built many organizations, only God can develop spiritual maturity. The hope of the spiritual leader is that the Spirit of God will so permeate his life and ministry that the casual observer will not comment, "What a church!" Instead he rejoices, "What a Saviour!" If this sensitivity to God is not honed, then a sincere spiritual leader may seek for acceptance, affirmation and significance from those he leads rather than looking to Christ where our legitimate spiritual needs are fulfilled.

Perspective is only gained when we willingly and consciously reject the idolatry of pride, selfish ambition and any other pursuit of fleshly origin and choose instead to experience the unconditional love and grace of God at work in us and through us. It is a sound prediction that grace, which is sufficient for today, will not be sufficient for tomorrow. That is why we must daily seek God's grace, which is always sufficient.

In fact, it is this private everyday relationship with Christ that is the key to effective public leadership. Hebrews 13:10–12 exhorts,

"We have an altar, whereof they have no right to eat which serve the tabernacle. For the bodies of those beasts, whose blood is brought into the sanctuary by the high priest for sin, are burned without the camp. Wherefore Jesus also, that he might sanctify the people with his own blood, suffered without the gate."

I love the phrase **"we have an altar."** I have memories from childhood of preachers inviting people to the altar for prayer, and I have experienced moments of healing, conviction and direction at an altar, as have many others. However, we acknowledge that our true Altar is the Person of the Lord Jesus Christ! Just as eternal life is not a place but a Person,[9] so our altar is not merely stairs leading up to the platform in our churches but the Person of the Lord Jesus Christ Himself. As we daily worship Him in prayer and service, our hearts are established in grace. We must not substitute our worship of Christ with a church, a person or any religious organization.

Another interesting phrase in Hebrews 13:13 is **"without the camp."** First-century Hebrew Christians were challenged to leave Judaism and follow Christ. Godly leaders have a parallel calling. It is a call to **true**

discipleship—a following after Christ with all of our heart, soul, mind and strength. Even as the Old Testament *sin offering* was burned *outside of the camp,* so also Jesus was crucified for our sins outside the walls of Jerusalem. Today He calls leaders to follow Him down a path that is not attractive, easy or popular because it leads 'outside the camp.' One who chooses to follow Jesus soon finds that the joy of **KNOWING HIM** and His grace is the supreme privilege of serving.

The plague of the generations is service and ministry that do not flow from a heart of grace, from a heart that knows Him. The result is that the world and the church do not see a genuine Christian experience in the lives of those who bear the name of Christ. Consequently, they do not perceive their own need to call upon Him or serve Him. A leader with a heart undeveloped in the discipline of grace will lose his focus and lose his desire to *see God.* His memory that such an experience is possible will grow dim, and if a vision is even possible for that man or his flock, it will be vague indeed. When the vision finally does perish, so will the people spiritually. One may talk of good works and giving, but these acts of service can flow only from hearts enlisted in the service of grace.

The practical outworking of this grace is exercised in the use of our spiritual gifts. Spiritual gifts are exciting. Not only has God saved us, but He has also equipped us to serve Him. These gifts have their origin in divine grace through the Holy Spirit. They are administered differently to believers in order that a Christian's "gift mix" will complement instead of compete with the "gift mixes" of other Christians in the local church.

Another aspect of spiritual gifts is that they are the means by which we are able to fulfill one of the great commandments, "that we should believe on the name of his Son Jesus Christ, **and LOVE ONE ANOTHER.**" [10]

Peter affirms that we love one another by exercising our gifts, for they were given for the benefit of the church body, not personal gain or profit. We see as we read I Corinthians 12 and Romans 12 that there are at least eleven permanent, edifying gifts legitimately at work in the church today, which can be listed in separate categories:

Speaking Gifts	*Nonverbal Gifts*
Prophecy	**RULING**
Knowledge	Helps
Wisdom	Giving
Teaching	Mercy
Exhortation	Faith
	Discernment

Take note of the first gift listed in the nonverbal column. God's Word addresses those who rule or lead, instructing that they should do so with diligence.[11]

God has gifted local churches with ample leadership, and these leaders must be allowed to lead **with diligence.** Across America, there are blessed ministries where God's servant leaders minister to people who appreciate their gift(s). On the other hand, hundreds of churches of unbiblical machinery and hierarchy handcuff God-ordained and gifted leaders. Others are not bound by ecclesiastical restraints; however, an unforgiving memory of interpersonal conflict and possibly failure haunts and limits their present ministerial efforts. These reasons, although compelling, are invalid. Truth calls men of God to serve Him and to serve others in leadership. It is vital that spiritual leadership be identified and permitted to lead the local church.

Leadership is a spiritual gift of grace. Peter exhorts, "As every man hath received the gift, even so minister the same one to another, as good stewards of the **MANIFOLD GRACE OF GOD.**"[12] Our spiritual gifts are

GRACE GIFTS intended for the benefit of the local church and the consecration of our personal lives. These gifts from the treasury of God's grace overflow our lives with blessing, purpose and potential. True spiritual leadership begins, continues and concludes by the grace of God. It is only by His grace that we are privileged and enabled to serve.

When our service extends from a heart disciplined by grace, we serve with joy. If we allow any competing motivation to produce our service, we will lose our effectiveness and possibly the privilege of leadership too. Therefore, let us keep before us the admonition that leaders who are guided by grace magnify Christ—not buildings, programs or people, and certainly not ourselves. Motive is a subtle and difficult animal to train, yet it influences all our lives. So let us pray that the sanctifying grace of Christ alone will establish and motivate us. He builds leaders contrary to the world's model, and the tool of His instruction is grace.

CHAPTER 2

Wanted: Servant Leaders

How I praise Thee, precious Saviour,
    That Thy Love laid hold of me;
Thou hast saved and cleansed and filled me
    That I might Thy channel be.

Channels only, blessed Master,
    But with all Thy wondrous pow'r
Flowing thru us, Thou canst use us
    Ev'ry day and ev'ry hour.[1]

If one decided to advertise in the classified section of his local newspaper in search of leaders, what characteristics and qualities should he list in the ad? One person attempting such a task submitted,

> HELP WANTED: SERVANT—Someone to do often undesirable work for the sake of others. Needs strong sense of [worth] in God's eyes and true compassion for others. Must be personally acquainted with the greatest Servant of all in order to continue his training. Work requires being on call 24 hours a day to meet needs of family, friends and even strangers. Must be willing to give up his rights—no experience necessary—job begins today, right where you are.[2]

A spiritual leader is one who determines that he will follow after the Person of the Lord Jesus Christ in each circumstance and relationship of life. He constantly "[looks] unto Jesus the author and finisher of [his] faith."[3] This submission to **lead by following** requires a daily decision, yet the promises of such devotion invite the investment. The Apostle John rejoiced in such a promise when he penned, "If ye abide in me, and my words abide in you, ye shall ask what ye will, and it shall be done unto you."[4] Notice the "if" clause in this verse, which indicates a choice. We are responsible to follow Him as we lead others.

The Apostle Paul repeatedly spoke of himself as a bond-servant of Jesus Christ. It is only in the consistency and context of this relationship that Paul was able to invite his flock to be "followers of me, even as I also am of Christ."[5]

Pastors are confronted with increasing ministry challenges. In the midst of this, there is a development on the part of some to infuse secular management principles into Christian ministries without holding them up to the light of God's Word. While not all principles exercised in the secular world are unscriptural, it is wise to reflect that *managers* are people who do things right, but *leaders* are servants who do the right thing; and for *spiritual leaders,* **the right thing** is to follow Jesus Christ.

Jesus is the model for servant leadership. Our humanity ensures us that we will fall "short of the glory of God";[6] however, we must pursue His example and **look to Him alone** as the model for our personal ministries.

The Gospels provide us with an eyewitness account of His actions and a glimpse at His motive; however, it is the Apostle Paul who provides us with insight into the heart and mind attitude of the Saviour, which enabled the Lord to finish the assignment given by His Father. Paul reveals that,

> "[Jesus] *made himself of no reputation, and took upon him the form of a servant, and was made in the likeness of men: And being found in fashion as a man, he humbled himself, and became*

obedient unto death, even the death of the cross. Wherefore God also hath highly exalted him, and given him a name which is above every name."[7]

This passage demonstrates with clarity that Jesus never laid aside His deity during His earthly ministry; rather, He emptied Himself of the prerogatives of His deity that He might offer redemption to a lost and depraved human race. The King of Kings **made Himself** of no reputation. He never demanded the authority or position that were rightfully His.

Meditations upon the great passion and humility of Christ convince one that true authority is never grasped. God's hand is active and evident in the life of the leader who diligently serves his people, thereby earning, rather than requiring, their respect. The Great Servant Leader possessed rather than commanded. His authority and status were attained in relationship with His Father rather than in response to the whims of the people. "**For Christ Alone**" is the marching order for the spiritual leader, and yet experience teaches that people will judge and misinterpret the motives of the leader whose ministry is blessed and growing. Some even speak against God's servants and accuse them of seeking status; however, it is a comfort to know that it is the Lord of Lords, also misunderstood and rejected by men, who knows us, sees us and examines our hearts' attitudes toward Him.

With these realities before us, let the godly leader beware of preoccupation with numerical graphs and shun his human desire to speak at a particular conference or be recognized in some public capacity. This is only possible when we die to self and self-ambition. Playing the political game in ministry can only cause regret. Instead, let our prayers reflect those of the man who was after God's own heart:

"Thou art my portion, O LORD: I have said that I would keep thy words. I intreated thy favour with my whole heart: be merciful unto me according to thy word."[8]

Some years ago I was privileged to spend time with Dr. Lee Roberson of Chattanooga, Tennessee. Dr. Roberson served as pastor for forty-one years at the Highland Park Baptist Church and founded Tennessee Temple Schools. Over the years God has used him to baptize more than 60,000 converts. The university has trained men and women who are dispersed around the world bearing the testimony and reproach of Christ for His name's sake.

On this occasion we enjoyed a conversation, the memory of which still challenges me. I asked him, "Dr. Roberson, can you give me some guidance or some hint as to how you were able to pastor such a great work for over forty years?"

His answer was short yet profound. He said, "**You must learn to die to self. Die to criticism and die to compliments. Then you may have the filling of the Holy Spirit.**"

I have sought diligently to apply this truth to my life. When I have succeeded, God's blessing has been affirmed. Conversely, when I have failed, heartache has been the result. It has been my experience that as we determine to die to ourselves and to make ourselves of no reputation, we approach the reality of serving as a leader.

Jesus voluntarily **took upon Himself** the form of a servant on our behalf. From this viewpoint, Jesus instructed His disciples, saying,

"Ye know that the princes of the Gentiles exercise dominion over them, and they that are great exercise authority upon them. But it shall not be so among you: but whosoever will be great among you, let him be your minister; And whosoever will be chief among you, let him be your servant: Even as the Son of man came not to be ministered unto, but to minister, and to give his life a ransom for many."[9]

Will we answer the call to God's kind of greatness or to the world's kind of greatness? We are not called to organize or administrate. We are called to gird ourselves with a towel and wash feet. **Our service is the measure of our greatness!** The Apostle Paul applied this principle as he ministered to the Corinthians. He emphasized the importance of servant leadership when he addressed their tendency to attach importance to themselves by identifying with a popular leader in an inordinate way. He admonished them by writing, "For while one saith, I am of Paul; and another, I am of Apollos; are ye not carnal?" [10] Paul took the opportunity to define his role and position among them, stating, "Let a man so account of [me], as of the [minister] of Christ." [11] As we learn to follow the Servant Leader, we will refrain from seeking our own status and serve voluntarily.

The paradox of the ages is that the Christ was born in a stable among animals and during His earthly ministry had no place to lay His head. Such circumstances did not keep Him from ministering to those in need. Jesus may have qualified for welfare, had it operated in His day: surely His works were not prompted by His means. In fact, His ministry to those in need existed because **He was made in fashion as a man.**

More is to be discovered from this key phrase than evidence of the incarnation. This supreme example of servant leadership confirms the will of God in this matter. Paul translated its application for us when he said,

"For though I be free from all men, yet have I made myself servant unto all, that I might gain the more."

"I am made all things to all men, that I might by all means save some. And this I do for the gospel's sake, that I might be partaker thereof with you." [12]

A leader who follows Christ's example adopts the mind of Christ and willingly departs from his comfort zone that he may gain the more for the sake of the Gospel. This may include visiting the shut-ins and those in need or praying with a brokenhearted family. A servant leader recognizes the needs and responds with the heart and mind of Christ.

An account of missionary statesman Hudson Taylor, pioneer missionary to inland China, mentions two young missionaries newly arrived on the field. To their dismay, there was a backup of the sewer line on the missionary compound where they lived, and the problem was becoming serious. The two younger missionaries stood over the pit, looking at the refuse and arguing with one another. The first man pointed to his credentials to excuse him from the dirty task, while the other tried to pull rank, citing that he was older. Their contention grew as they armed themselves with increased reasons why they should not descend into the pit of sewage to remedy the problem, which was becoming worse with each passing moment.

In their preoccupation with themselves and their rights, they didn't notice when Hudson Taylor himself climbed into the pit of sewage and removed the matter that had created the problem. He then climbed out and went back to work. This account illustrates well that immature leaders will rationalize to excuse themselves from hard ministry, while mature leaders see the need and then take the lead.

CHAPTER 3

A Model Who Works

"He riseth from supper, and laid aside his garments; and took a towel, and girded himself. After that he poureth water into a bason, and began to wash the disciples' feet, and to wipe them with the towel." [1]

I am the first to recommend Christian service, specifically pastoral leadership, as a worthy life investment, and quick to praise God for the privilege of His having put me into the ministry. Grace-filled moments complemented by life-changing relationships with people whose influence has caused me to become a better person are only a part of the reward of ministry. However, any consideration of ministry must include this detail: ministry is hard work. By its very nature it is God-centered rather than self-centered. Paul testified that he did not seek glory from men, from those whom he served or others. In fact, his ministry focused upon the promotion of God's purposes and the spiritual development of believers. Jesus and Paul were models who worked. We should follow their example.

Paul frequently made reference to the labor of ministry, drawing an analogy in Galatians worth noting. He wrote, "My little children, of whom I travail in birth again until Christ be formed in you." [2] Paul's reference to the labor of ministry evoked the mental image of a woman in childbirth.

Some years ago a popular comedian shared that giving birth was like taking your bottom lip and pulling it up over your head—not an easy task. However, due to his reliance upon God, Paul maintained a remarkably positive outlook and steadfast determination to minister amidst the conflict and pain. Paul knew he was not alone in the ministry, even when "no man stood with [him.]"[3] He recognized that "neither is he that planteth any thing, neither he that watereth; but God [is the One that gives] the increase. Now he that planteth and he that watereth are one: and every man shall receive his own reward according to his own labour. For we are labourers together with God."[4]

Evidence abounds that this apostle did not entertain any ministry misconceptions. He knew the hard work of service. He was intimately acquainted with both the physical labors and the more intense mental and emotional labors that a servant leader must work through, placing the spiritual enlargement of others before himself, not once but as a pattern of daily life. The minister's work is inward preparation, not outward performance, as Paul indicated to Timothy, commanding him to take heed to the disciplines of his own spiritual life and to the doctrine. "The preacher's first and most important task is to prepare himself, not his sermon."[5]

Paul instructed Timothy that a man desiring the office of pastor desired a **good work**; likewise, servant leadership today requires good, hard work. Is that what we envisioned when we considered the ministry? Hard work? Paul clearly communicates to the Thessalonian believers that his audience, the witness and judge of his labors, was God alone. Our highest aim is to please Him.

Some years ago I accepted an invitation to speak at a particular conference. As the host introduced me, he mentioned the numerical size of our ministry in various categories. His information was off (low) in every category. I regret thinking, *Doesn't he know that our ministry is larger than that?* At the same moment, there came the swift and searching conviction of the Holy Spirit: *Does it really matter? Whom exactly are you trying to impress?*

While we may believe that numerical growth in a church is **one** indication of God's blessing, we must understand that true success in spiritual leadership is formed as we are faithful to the Saviour. We could say that God, who adds to the church, is not as interested in the size of a church as He is in the spiritual health of a church.

It is vital to the health of spiritual leadership that we render our service unto Him alone. Success is a moving target; but leadership, a fixed goal; and that goal is to please Him. Falling into the trap to please men never satisfies. The tragedy is that many gifted and called men are codependent on the praise of people rather than fully dependent on Christ. This type of codependency, based on flattery and praise, can lead to a number of sins, including depression, foolish jesting, even immorality. One *motion* each of us must personally make is a *demotion;* and in that place of humility, we join in the sober but necessary affirmation "He must increase, but I must decrease."[6]

This decrease is possible only when we trust in God who has our best interests at heart—a God who has the ability and intention to enrich our most vulnerable moments with glory and growth in His grace. The evidence of this glory is that God's people *fix their eyes upon Jesus.* They trust Him, learn more of Him, draw closer to Him and worship Him. Such focus lends both purpose and peace to our most difficult circumstances.

Our congregation in Lancaster experienced this growth through the circumstances of one of our staff members recently. A few years ago Dave and Lori, a young couple, joined our ministry staff. Just as they were getting their feet planted in the ministry, Lori learned from her doctor that she was terminally ill. Her diagnosis began a great spiritual and physical battle against the cancer. Lori died recently. She passed into eternity with more grace than anyone else I have ever seen, without exception. Truly Lori became an instrument of God's glory.

One of Lori's responsibilities had been to contact new Christians and enroll them in our church discipleship program. Consequently, she had encouraged hundreds of new believers during her years with us. Many of our members and I had been at the hospital around the clock in the last weeks of her life. We prayed and sang and did our best to serve her family. As I ministered at Lori's funeral, I wondered at the impact that one woman had made in her short twenty-five-year life. Testimonies of letters and notes of encouragement, coupled with other intentional acts of kindness, had touched many of the 1,500 people who attended her service. People gave back that which they had received, demonstrating Christian love for Lori's husband and the rest of her family as they grieved.

Only God is capable of turning our tears into thanksgiving. The moving of the Holy Spirit upon the hearts of our church family has been so tremendous that it cannot be compared to numerical growth. I marvel at His grace—at His ability to transform our trials into glory and growth.

Lori was a servant. Her unfeigned love of Christ and commitment to work in the ministry was the basis of the appreciation she received. This exemplifies a pattern that was modeled by Paul as he ministered to the Thessalonians who grew in grace through trials because of the service of a committed worker. Even a cursory reading of these epistles is sufficient to reveal the radical change that took place in the lives of the Thessalonians after they believed, for they had turned from idols to the living God. Their confession was followed by a true conversion of character and conduct. Note also that their renewed conduct included an intense devotion to God and to the servant leader whom God had sent to them.

As Paul called these new believers to exercise all their rational powers, loving the Lord their God with all their heart, soul, mind and strength, they also developed an intense love for Paul and his labor among them. Paul records that they "became followers of [him], and of the Lord, having received the word in much affliction, with joy of the Holy Ghost."[7] So much was their devotion to Paul that in a letter to the Corinthians he boasts of their faithfulness to him and to God. He wrote,

> "Moveover, brethren, we do you to wit of the grace of God bestowed on the churches of Macedonia [of which Thessalonica was a part]; How that in a great trial of affliction the abundance of their joy and their deep poverty abounded unto the riches of their liberality. For to their power, I bear record, yea, and beyond their power they were willing of themselves; Praying us with much intreaty that we would receive the gift, and take upon us the fellowship of the ministering to the saints. And this they did, not as we hoped, but first gave their own selves to the Lord, and unto us by the will of God."[8]

This is surprising because in the Thessalonian Epistle Paul testifies that he never used flattering words, secretly abused them for greedy gain nor sought glory for himself. In fact, he recalls that his actions were purposefully gentle, motherly and affectionate as he worked day and night to impart both the Gospel and his life to these believers for their spiritual growth and benefit.

He then reveals the character of his motivation: holy, just, blameless and without respect to an earthly reward or recognition. Paul was just an ordinary man, albeit a committed one, who labored in the sacrifice and service of the Faith—delivering to people the engrafted Word that is able to save souls.

Thank God for the Epistle to the Thessalonians. It reminds us that we are not called to be clever wordsmiths, eloquent exegetes or salvation supermen—we are called to serve. We are called to love. We are responsible to study, pray and prepare—to exercise our spiritual gifts within the framework of our calling.

In this Thessalonian case study, clearly it was not Paul but rather the force of the gospel message delivered faithfully which resulted in an intense devotion of the people to their servant leader and to the doctrine. And their faith became known in every place and abroad. The force of the Gospel of grace transformed the character of the Thessalonian people. However, it was the manner of communication of that gospel force which served as the agent of that change, and men whom God had put in trust with the Gospel rendered that service.

We can discipline ourselves to communicate the Gospel faithfully, lovingly and without apology. In other words, we can work, but we cannot control the results. We rest in God's promise to bring forth fruit from our labors.

Paul trusted God, believing that his ministry was not in vain, and by faith saw the evidence of the Spirit's continuing work—developing the faith of the Thessalonian believers and setting apart certain ones for training in the service of leadership. Paul, uniquely ordained by God to equip leaders, soberly taught these men the Scriptures, their responsibilities and the privileges of ministry. However, he also exhorted believers to know those who labored among them, who exercised authority in the Lord, "and to esteem them very highly in love for their work's sake."[9] The relationship between the servant leader and the people was reciprocal.

The instruction to the leaders was binding, and they were subject to accountability; likewise, the respect due them for their service was framed in language corresponding to the giving of an order, an expression of duty. This esteem was equally binding and subject to accountability. However, the respect given a pastor was not token esteem. It was genuine thanksgiving for the ministry of a pastor whose communication of the Gospel lovingly moved believers toward more consecrated lives and the further development of both their individual and collective spiritual character. Paul knew that if leaders were truly servants, then the high esteem taught as the duty of believers would in fact be the delight and natural emotional response of the people.

Emotion in ministry begins in the heart, in the context of a love relationship with God. From Him flows the ability to love, accept, forgive, teach and equip—in other words, to oversee the spiritual development of others—to serve them. "Servanthood as a leadership style does not mean we forfeit the administrative functions commanded in Scripture and seen in Christ's example."[10] The pastor is called to be the key administrator. The phrase "over you in the Lord" appears three times in the Pastoral Epistles, and it succinctly defines the role of the servant leader in the local church.

Hebrews 13:17 warns also that pastors will give a personal account before the Lord for the spiritual oversight which they have rendered and the message they have delivered, but their message and oversight are not a matter of words alone.

Servant leaders communicate the force of the Gospel effectively because their hard work and devotion model the love and forgiveness they preach. They are not looking out for their own welfare or seeking their own interests; rather, they genuinely care for the souls of men. They do not represent themselves but Christ. They are ambassadors, ministers of reconciliation, who boldly confess, "I preach not myself but Jesus Christ and Him crucified."

The role of a pastor is not to read one verse and then tell stories about his life or give commentary on current events for an hour. A periodic illustration can be helpful, but it is the faithful delivery of a Christ-centered message by a man with God-centered motives that is the ultimate act of love in leadership. Yes, we have been entrusted with oversight, but that oversight is exercised *in the Lord.* **"It is an earned leadership forged in relationships: first, the pastor's relationship with the Lord and, second, the pastor's relationship to his people."** [11] Thus the pastor's authority is first endued upon him by God, and then it is earned as he faithfully and humbly serves the people. It is commonly accepted that service and leadership are different roles which must be exercised in a balanced manner. I submit to you that leadership is service. We must be models who work. Only then will the church be equipped to function properly and the people enabled to fulfill the purposes and loving intentions of the Lord for their lives, which will include loving their pastor.

Section 2

21st-Century Leadership
Challenges

CHAPTER 4

Go Forward

Day by day and with each passing moment,
   Strength I find to meet my trials here;
Trusting in my Father's wise bestowment,
   I've no cause for worry or for fear.
He whose heart is kind beyond all measure
   Gives unto each day what He deems best—
Lovingly, its part of pain and pleasure,
   Mingling toil with peace and rest.[1]

J.F.K. Airport 1992: We landed, navigated our way through the circus of baggage claim and joined some friends who warmly welcomed us to New York. My wife, Terrie, and I were excited about the preaching conference where I would speak, being able to spend time together while taking in some New England sights. We rented a car and began our adventure; however, we were soon trapped in a maze of gridlock near Madison Square Garden, indicating something big was scheduled for the evening. We spent the next hour at a standstill, taking in rather than visiting the sights. The big event turned out to be the Democratic National Convention. We watched as a parade of people, issues and outright wickedness passed by our imprisoned car.

The colorful parade grieved us. There were women and men lewdly dancing atop a semi-truck labeled "Teamsters." Pro-abortion chants by supporters vying; gay-rights streamers and rainbow flags flying. The music pulsated loud enough to deaden the senses with Fleet-wood Mac's "Don't Stop Thinking About Tomorrow" inciting the crowd. People found or fashioned platforms and denounced Bush and Quayle in the streets. What was the charge? Bill Clinton stated it in his speech later that night, and it became a key phrase in the Clinton campaign: "Bush/Quayle are a ticket to the past, but our ticket is a ticket to the future."

How is it that Americans are knowingly rejecting the godly values of our past? We now live in the reality of those past promises. Is this "that future" that the American people thought they were buying a ticket for? Rejection of traditional values is devouring our society and churches. As a result, conservative politics and churches alike struggle to be "relevant" in an irreligious culture. Pragmatism prevails, and truth is deemed relative.

The wisest of men once cautioned, "Buy the truth, and sell it not."[2] Likewise, a godly pastor will grow and change because he is continually being conformed to the image and mind of Christ instead of the image and mind of the world.

Terrie and I eventually freed ourselves from the traffic outside the Madison Square Garden; but later in the week, en route to Vermont, we decided to stop in North-field, Massachusetts, the birthplace of D. L. Moody. Having heard of Moody since childhood, I was eager to visit his birthplace and conference grounds.

To my surprise, it was difficult to find students at the school who knew who Moody was. In addition, we could not find anyone to share our excitement about seeing his birthplace. Finally, an elderly man walked us to the restored home of Moody's birthplace. While inside I marveled at the Bibles of Moody, the notes he had sent to his family and the names of the men who had preached at Northfield. After spending an hour or so looking at Moody memorabilia, we strolled through the campus and back to our car. While walking, I saw the man who had made the special effort to let us into the Moody house. I approached him and thanked him for his kindness to us and was intrigued when he mentioned that Moody was his great-uncle. I asked him a few questions about the ministry of Moody but was stopped rather abruptly. He assumed that I "wouldn't have liked D. L. Moody. He was too authoritative and too narrow-minded." We thanked him again for his time as we continued our drive north. We realized that although we may have loved Moody's style, the average American Christian today would probably view him with suspicion and consider his manner both harsh and abrasive.

Yes, suspicion abounds today. In fact, one may clearly observe in the world our society's growing disdain for absolutes and authority. Because of this, leaders—spiritual leaders in particular—are targets of cynical scrutiny. Our position as pastors does not warrant respect, only suspicion.

Strong Bible-based ministry has become unpopular. An increasing segment of the American population suspects that believers of the Bible are intolerant and cultic. Such perceptions challenge contemporary servant leaders, and it is in their best interest to acquaint themselves with the reasons why so many people, saved and unsaved alike, are sincerely suspicious of ministers and ministry today.

What causes comments such as I heard from one lady, "I just don't believe a church can grow without being corrupt"? Well, in some sense, every church, no matter the size of its congregation, will have sin, imperfection and, yes, corruption, if its members are people. However, some people's feelings run deeper than the old "too many hypocrites in church for me" line of defense. Some of their false perceptions arise from outside influences, while others are founded in the past or present failures of a leader and his lack of growth and grace.

Each individual views church and ministers through the paradigm of his own life experiences, which often results in confusion. Now we know that the author of confusion and lies is Satan himself; however, there are other contributing factors which promote these false perceptions:

1. media portrayal of ministers;
2. proliferation of religious cults;
3. secular humanism and the New Age movement;
4. failure of Christian leaders;
5. unbelievers' control of some "Christian" publishing houses;
6. imbalances and abusive ministries.

Christian-bashing in the media is certainly nothing new. The early seventies brought a wave of programming and movies which portrayed preachers as overbearing, self-serving gluttons. In addition, Christian values are ridiculed by companies which were previously trusted, such as Disney. Some movies, such as *The Last Temptation of Christ,* even question the virtue and deity of the Lord Himself.

One CBS production featured a story about a church that was labeled "controlling" because it was opposed to conventional psychotherapy. The main character in the show was a man who was trying to alienate his wife from their kids and encouraged her to attempt suicide. He, of course, was a leader in the church. The main deacon also was arrested for spying on a policeman and not paying back child support. His name, interestingly, was the same as conservative columnist Alan Keyes.

A second factor that affects the current religious climate in America is a rise in the number of questionable religious cults. The Bible teaches that a Christian should live a distinct and godly walk **in society.** In contrast, cultic groups tend to cause people to **disconnect from society**, and over time the adherents also become disconnected from certain realities of life. Whether it is Sun Myung Moon, the self-proclaimed Messiah; Jim Jones or David Koresh, the proliferation of cults in today's society leaves a bad taste in the mouths of many with respect to religion.

Those of us who have studied the Word of God are not shocked by the rise in the number of these self-proclaimed "Christs" and their followers. First John 2:18 warns, "Little children, it is the last time: and as ye have heard that antichrist shall come, even now are there many antichrists; whereby we know that it is the last time."

The cult movements are accompanied by what the Bible refers to as a great spirit of apostasy that will abound in the last days—these days. Men and women are denying that truth even exists, leaving Bible-teaching churches and turning to the New Age movement in unprecedented numbers. In fact, some entire congregations today have forsaken sound Bible doctrine for messages on subjects ranging from environmentalism to the New World Order. The Bible speaks of this apostasy in Jude 3 and 4:

"Beloved, when I gave all diligence to write unto you of the common salvation, it was needful for me to write unto you, and exhort you that ye should earnestly contend for the faith which was once delivered unto the saints. For there are certain men crept in unawares, who were before of old ordained to this condemnation, ungodly men, turning the grace of our God into lasciviousness, and denying the only Lord God, and our Lord Jesus Christ."

Truly the tragedy of the cults and apostate teachings of the New Age movement are being used by Satan to cast doubt in some people's minds about all religion.

A third contributing factor toward the growing mistrust of ministry is the increasing rise of secular humanism and New Age doctrines. Humanism and the

New Age movement propagate the concept of over-turning authority. Both of these philosophies promote man as his own authority; man's reason is exalted. Like Eve in the Garden of Eden, man is deceived. He thinks that he can or has become like God. As a result, one's need for a personal Saviour such as Jesus Christ is rendered obsolete. This emphasis on one's self as the final authority affects the world's perspective of Christianity more than we would like to admit.

The pride-based philosophy of humanism and New Age creeds is not new. The battle against God's authority began with Lucifer's revolt against God.

"How art thou fallen from heaven, O Lucifer, son of the morning! how art thou cut down to the ground, which didst weaken the nations! For thou hast said in thine heart, I will ascend into heaven, I will exalt my throne above the stars of God: I will sit also upon the mount of the congregation, in the sides of the north: I will ascend above the heights of the clouds; I will be like the most High."[3]

Later Satan deceived Eve, promising what he could not achieve nor deliver in the shape, form and scent of a forbidden fruit: godlikeness. Adam joined in this disobedience; and so each succeeding generation is equally subject to the same temptation now disguised in the language of humanism, which asserts, "You can be your own God." Christians who have been exposed to humanistic educational philosophies are especially susceptible to these subconscious influences. But our God is worthy of praise; for He renews our minds, redeeming us not merely from the physical grave but also from the sepulcher of dead thoughts that shaped our minds and wills before we believed.

Thus we see the current manifestations of humanism that are against God and against authority, even parental authority. The humanist influence permeates the public schools of America. One California news station aired a report that ninth graders in a human interaction program were sent home with work sheets that judged whether their families worked on an "open democratic" mold or a "closed authoritarian" model. I suppose a parent who insists a child should make his bed would be judged too authoritarian.

A fourth instrument of similar force in the fall of Biblical Christianity in America has been the private sin, now public, of many prominent Christian leaders. Mature believers know to focus on Christ and to keep seeing Him; however, many bewildered believers and unbelievers are suspicious, and not without some cause. The moral failure of leaders from various denominations has affected all Christian leaders. In the past it was the gospel message that was disbelieved by the lost; and now, to the shame of the whole Christian community, it is the messenger whose integrity and purity are questioned.

The purchasing of "Christian" publishing houses by nonbelievers also mixes up already muddy waters. Sincere seekers of truth visiting a Christian bookstore today are woefully unable to discern which books represent authentic Christian leadership and doctrine. Nonbelieving or theologically liberal editors now edit many books covering subjects such as grace, church administration and Christian living in order that publishing houses may appeal to the broadest market possible. Consequently, some Christian publications have undermined and are continuing to undermine church leadership indirectly by promoting unscriptural philosophies.

A prime example of the danger of unregenerate ownership of "Christian" publishing houses occurred when Zondervan was purchased in 1988 by Harper-Collins. Australian billionaire Rupert Murdoch owns the Harper-Collins publishing house. Murdoch also owns the Fox Television Network and several other companies. I have a Zondervan book on my library shelf printed in the 1950s entitled *The Danger of the Movie Theatre*. Could you imagine Zondervan publishing a title like that today, with or without Murdoch at the helm?

World magazine made the following observation about secular ownership:

> Church-related companies can ask questions about employee faith, but publicly held companies are not allowed to discriminate on the basis of religion. Christian ministries are often concerned with doctrinal fidelity, but secular corporations are motivated mainly by the bottom line.[4]

Unfortunately, the bottom line today is that strong doctrine and strong Biblical leadership concepts are not going to sell. Basically, the larger publishing companies are following the market trends rather than endeavoring to spread truth.

> Self-help is another popular category for evangelical publishers, despite the irony that self-help seems the opposite of historical emphases upon the grace of God. Many of these titles are little more than pop-psychology, which promotes standard secular beliefs such as self-esteem and assertiveness in ministry. Others approach the Bible itself as a self-help manual.[5]

A final and significant concern for the church and its leadership is abuse. We might think by listening to some that have been hurt in church-related ministries that another twelve-step program was needed for "recovering churchgoers." While some of the claims of abuse may be questionable, leaders must be willing to evaluate their ministry philosophy and practices in the light of Scripture—confirming that God's grace is both evident and working in their churches. However, I also believe there are abusive leadership styles and techniques that should be avoided if our desire is to foster an environment of servant leadership in the church.

Godly leadership and authority are conferred by God

and must not be grasped or seized. An effective spiritual leader will always lead from a position of authority, but we must keep in mind that the authority is a gift from God and not something earned for self or self-gratification. Such fleshly approaches to leadership birth a critical, self-promoting spirit in the church, born of the leader and imitated by the people. This in turn creates an environment of competition, division and dissension of which the shepherd himself is the instigator.

As a young pastor, I attended some meetings where critical, self-promoting styles were modeled. I thank the Lord for the Biblical truths I heard from those pastors— but looking back, I can see that often the speakers' castigation or shameful statements appealed to my carnal nature. I am a fundamental, Bible-believing pastor and know that I am to reprove, rebuke and exhort. Yet I must do this boldly **in doctrine** and patiently **in love**. This is a tough balance for all preachers, but we must never single out any individual over an issue that should remain a private matter.

It is interesting to observe that the more caustic leaders and speakers generate a like spirit in their followers. We can observe these pastors biting and devouring their own mentors. Personally, I love red-hot preaching—so long as the Bible principle clearly supports the subject; but we do not need to promote a competitive, divisive spirit in our churches or pastors' meetings.

There may be times when a pastor will, from the pulpit, deal with an issue that is widespread in the church, but we should avoid using the pulpit to address a problem with an individual that would be better dealt with in a one-on-one setting.

One mistake to avoid is generalizing illustrations. For example, a pastor can say, "I know of a man who years ago took great offense at a church decision." This broad statement could cause defensive feelings with more than one man in the congregation who spends the rest of the sermon guessing who the mystery man is or wondering if the preacher was referring to him.

Another caution in public speaking is to endeavor to clear your mind from the heavy counseling load from the week prior to preaching. I have on a few occasions had something from my subconscious mind slip into a message or conversation. Although I have never named someone by name, I have always felt grieved and wished I had expressed the point in the message or communication differently. After all, it is the pastor's responsibility to be a peacemaker and to model grace and forgiveness in the congregation. Obviously, it is never right to use the pulpit to berate individuals in the congregation. This practice never comes to a fruitful end, and because this does happen, some Christians hold ministers in suspicion.

Sometimes a well-intentioned pastor can come across as abusive in his verbal ministry because of his own feelings of insecurity. A good parallel is marriage. A young new husband eager to lead the home can easily quench the spirit of his new bride. Pastors who have not discovered their total acceptance in Christ and who seek significance in ministry rather than in Jesus will experience constant restlessness of spirit. This restless spirit and need for significance will often result in the establishing of unrealistic expectations for themselves and others, which may be expressed through controlling behaviors.

God's love and grace must motivate the spiritual leader. Otherwise, he will adversely affect the spiritual development of those he is called to serve. He will easily lose touch with the mind of God for the vision and pace of the ministry.

An obvious Biblical example of a man who abused his power in a prideful moment is King David. The book of II Samuel records that David obviously lost focus on God's call for his life. Notice several steps in his abuse of power:

(1) David neglected his role but expected others to fulfill theirs: In II Samuel 11:1, David excused himself from the battle by sending Joab in his place. However, Joab could not take his place, nor could he bear David's guilt when David asked him to send Uriah to the front lines. As leaders, we must fulfill our roles as pastors, husbands and fathers consistently as an encouragement for others to follow.

(2) David did not *serve* his people; he *manipulated* them: David's bad judgment call concerning the battle quickly elevated to gross sin when he called the beautiful Bathsheba to his adulterous bed. Abuse always involves using and manipulating people, and it is usually followed by poor rationalizations.

(3) David did not acknowledge his sin: There is something both sad and ugly about a man who cannot admit when he is wrong. David fell into this prideful trap and planned a heroic demise for the husband of Bathsheba. Finally, God sent Nathan to accuse David of his hypocrisy. Following this, God taught David a lesson, but it was a hard and bitter lesson. God will do the same to leaders who ill use their positions today. God is patient, but He is also just. The Lord is the Good Shepherd, and He will protect His sheep from abusive undershepherds.

Abusive ministry is probably not as widespread as some would like to think, but it is true that every pastor and spiritual leader must open his heart before God on a daily basis and acknowledge His authority in his life. We must die to self-will and seek to be alive in Christ as we serve His people.

Spiritual leaders must maintain obedience to the fixed authority in their lives—the Lord Jesus Christ. If we fail to submit to Him, we provoke the already suspicious public which seems eager to identify inconsistencies in leadership.

Ironically, many Christian psychologists and authors of the 1990s discovered a market among those who were hurting. Soon followed a proliferation of books and materials published on subjects related to abuse, which caused their readers to dwell upon their distrust instead of trusting in the healing and forgiveness of Christ.

A comforting and miraculous fact is that our God is the living God of the past, present and future. He owns time. We cannot go back in time and recover or soothe our past emotional distress, but the God who creates and keeps time can be active in our past, present and future simultaneously, shaping us into the instrument of His choosing by using our experiences for His glory. Adversely, "Satan likes us best when we are completely absorbed in trying to figure ourselves out, because at such moments, all forward motion stops."[6] As J. Oswald Sanders once stated, "Peace is not the absence of trouble, but the presence of God."[7]

The result of the present-day climate of suspicion has been both positive and negative. Positively, Christian ministries and spiritual leaders are taking regular spiritual inventory of their motives and mode of ministry. The Apostle Paul did likewise, as indicated in I Thessalonians, chapter 2. He began his personal inventory in verses 1 and 2 in which he called upon the Thessalonian believers as witnesses that his "entrance in unto [them],...was not in vain" and that he had been "bold in our God to speak unto [them] the gospel of God with much contention."

He continues his personal evaluation, specifying that his "exhortation was not of deceit, nor of uncleanness, nor in guile: But as [he had been] allowed of God to be put in trust with the gospel, even so [he had spoken]; not as pleasing men, but God, which trieth [the] hearts."[8] He brought to their remembrance that he had not "used...flattering words...nor a cloke of covetousness...Nor of men [did he seek] glory....[He was] gentle among [them], even as a nurse cherisheth her children...[for he was] willing to have imparted unto [them], not the gospel of God only, but also [his] own [soul], because [they] were dear unto [him]....[He labored] night and day, because [he] would not be chargeable unto any of [them], [he] preached unto [them] the gospel of God...[and he conducted himself] holily and justly and unblameably...: [he] exhorted and comforted and charged every one of [them], as a father doth his children."[9] Paul concluded his assessment, citing God as his witness.

Such assessments, which will be discussed later in this book, are established as both necessary and practical by Biblical precedent. A spiritual leader must constantly assess his motives and ministry so that they may reflect the heart, mind and vision of God for his life and for the life of the flock entrusted to him by God Himself.

The testimony of alleged victims of church abuse has produced negative results in and out of the body of Christ's believers: Within the body of Christ, many who were once victims are now victimizing their leaders. The suspicions and hostilities confronting spiritual leaders do not any longer exist only outside the four walls of the church. Some of our greatest opposition is in the pew. Their suspicions continue because they have not yet appropriated God's grace and forgiveness. The symptoms of their continued misery are manifest in three primary ways: they abuse spiritual leaders; they relabel ministry terms; they become unbalanced spiritually. They can't wait to tell the next pastor (and the next and the next one after that) about their difficulty in trusting pastoral leadership.

Satan is the author of lies and confusion; and I have no doubt that he delights in sending confusing signals with regard to spiritual leaders because he knows if someone will doubt the messenger, he will probably reject the message. Much of the confusion and suspicion of our day can be attributed to the Wicked One:

> *"For we wrestle not against flesh and blood, but against principalities, against powers, against the rulers of the darkness of this world, against spiritual wickedness in high places. Wherefore take unto you the whole armour of God, that ye may be able to withstand in the evil day, and having done all, to stand."*[10]

Our battle is not against people. We must prayerfully fight the Wicked One in the power of our resurrected Saviour.

In this confusing day, we have acknowledged that some in spiritual leadership have caused hurt, confusion and suspicion by their actions. Yet, sadly, many leaders today are also being hurt and maligned by those whom they have tried to serve. Many of those Christians who speak woefully against those in leadership claim they must do so because they would only be ridiculed or ignored if they went directly to a church leader; but this is often a smokescreen, for in reality most leaders would welcome an opportunity for a godly meeting in an effort to glorify Christ. Those in the reactionary paradigm seem to take pleasure in and feed on their self-appointed position of blame-thrower. However, God is not as interested in assigning blame as He is in resolving problems. His desire is reconciliation.

Spiritual leaders are not perfect people. They must be allowed to grow, and they should be willing to accept godly admonitions; but the angry and suspicious rarely allow for this growth; and while they talk of prayer and grace, their actions tend to be harsh and legalistic toward the leader. In fact, the very judgments and abuses they claim to have experienced are ammunition in their exploits to war against the authority of their spiritual leaders.

Detractors will always challenge the vision of leadership. We hear it in phrases like: "That little congregation will never accomplish that"; "They're just interested in numbers"; or "The pastor is on an ego trip." The leader must rise above such criticism. He must stand tall on his knees if he is to see above the crowd. The leader keeps vision alive and ensures the power of growth is ongoing.

Sometimes it is not the messenger that is despised or suspected as much as it is the message he preaches. Dr. John R. Rice advised:

> It is no strange thing that modern evangelists—that is, honest, Bible-preaching, Spirit-filled evangelists—these days are criticized and hated and abused. So it has always been with men of God who paid the price for revival! When men slandered Moody and called him "Crazy Moody," when men mocked at Billy Sunday's preaching and accused him of preaching for money, it was no more than should be expected by anyone who would follow in the steps of Elijah, seeking to prevail with God for revival.[11]

The Apostle Paul understood this price when he exhorted Timothy to "endure hardness, as a good soldier of Jesus Christ."[12]

The ridicule and abuse that leaders experience is not limited to a particular denomination. It is not limited to a particular leadership style. Wherever leaders lead Biblically, adversity will be present, and abuse will follow.

In my next comments, **I do not wish to endorse the ministry philosophy of any particular leader;** however, I think it interesting to note the common denominators of their experience. I have included comments about or by men from various backgrounds because each of them has been on the receiving end of statements intended to hurt or hinder his ministry.

The following statements were printed about a pastor in Virginia in *Christianity Today,* December 9, 1996: "...some **former supporters** say [he] has achieved his goals through a stifling authoritarianism, and that his organization's growth has been inhibited by his overly controlling methods."[13] Did you notice the quote was from "former supporters"? This man is certainly not perfect, but he does have thousands of former and present supporters and employees who appreciate his leadership and contributions. **Every ministry** in America—whether Baptist, Presbyterian, Pentecostal etc.—has some former supporters who would now disagree with their ministry. The insinuation is that this pastor's "controlling" methods were in some way unchristian.

One could define the word *controlling* as "asking someone to do what he or she doesn't want to do." Apparently these former supporters did not want to do something that their pastor had in mind or that he presented from the Word of God. Rather than simply stopping support of or leaving this church, they reacted with hurting innuendoes toward the ministry.

Later in the same article the author states, "...[This pastor] has convinced his followers that his word carries a special measure of authority."[14] Again the author of this ecumenical magazine article characterizes this man as a spiritual criminal who has convinced people of something that any leader could be accused of.

Another pastor in Texas provides an additional example. This man passed the mantle of his ministry to a "Timothy" after fifty years of serving as pastor. However, this "Timothy" proved both unfaithful and critical when he resigned his new post and disseminated a scathing report of his mentor's leadership. This depiction included words and phrases like "deceit" and "den of treachery." He even referred to his one-time mentor, now 84, as a conning, power-hungry tyrant.

While there may be those who aspire to leadership for the wrong reasons, this author highly doubts that this senior pastor faithfully preached and served for fifty years because of a lust for power nor due to selfish motives. Most men who become pastors of mega-churches have succeeded in the ministry because they inspire those around them to work in concert. The commitment necessary for such a task excludes a hunger for power and greed as legitimate motivations.

This retired pastor's fifty-year ministry must have been motivated by a love for Jesus. His critic has since divorced and remarried since his resignation and has shared that if he returns to the pulpit, it will be in a small church.

Again we see a man who was helped and mentored disagreeing and reacting in a less-than-graceful way. What was the result? The secular media reported of their difference, and the Devil sat in the corner laughing. Although the senior pastor resumed his preaching ministry, we have no doubt that he was grieved by this situation.

Another pastor in Phoenix, Arizona experienced incredible scrutiny and hurtful innuendo during a building program. He reveals in his book, "We became the talk of the town with a few even suggesting I was some wild cult leader with Jim Jones-like persuasion and a pocketful of money gleaned from foolish and duped attendees....it seemed everyone wanted to go public with their comments, whether they were based on facts or not." [15] This is one more example of a dynamic leader, serving to the best of his ability, being questioned and abused in his own community. Those who supported their pastor were referred to as being "duped," a common term appointed to those who appreciate the leadership models in their churches.

Again, a pastor in Atlanta reports in his book that some people in his church seemed concentrated on defaming him during a difficult time in his ministry. He remembers that "the next Wednesday night, which was a business meeting, I asked the church to give my Sunday school superintendent and me the full authority to appoint all the deacons and church officers. A member of the original opposition stood and gave a speech about how we were running him out of the church, and then he said, 'If you don't watch what you're doing, you're going to get hurt.' With that he hit me with the back of his hand in the face."[16] Perhaps this pastor's philosophy was not pleasing to a small group in the church, but the resulting defamation of character and physical assault by those who were suspicious of his intent were certainly not pleasing to Christ.

With these few examples in mind, we see a pattern developing that teaches us that spiritual leaders will be the recipients of the very tactics the suspicious and hurting claim they have received. "Yea, and all that will live godly in Christ Jesus shall suffer persecution."[17]

Those who hold a spiritual leader in suspicion will ultimately doubt everything about the leader's life and ministry. As a result of this suspicion a relabeling of ministry terms usually occurs:

Legitimate Terms	*Relabeled Terms*
preaching/teaching	bashing/shaming
decisive Biblical leadership	authoritarianism
local church	a system/organized religion
vision/direction	an agenda

While shameful pulpits where people are named and ridiculed do exist, another tragedy is developing. Specifically, cynically minded parishioners view all preaching as bashing, all strong leadership as authoritarian. The challenge is found in the fact that leadership that is not strong is not leadership at all. Often those who could justly benefit by the leadership of a parent or pastor never experience this benefit because of their false perceptions or personal rejection of spiritual leadership.

Many in our society and in our Christian culture today reject the absolute nature of the Christian Faith. Many desire spiritual experiences, choices, preferences and comfort instead of knowledge, absolutes, truth and growth. Such people prefer to make up their own way and their own faith instead of following the One who is the Way, the Truth and the Life.

Additionally, it is wrong to label a ministry that preaches the pure Gospel of grace as a "system" or "organized religion" that is merely following human agendas. These hurtful labels are carelessly thrown like grenades without regard for the church leader who happens to be in the path of the tiny weapon with the big blast.

Every ministry will reflect some of the weak human characteristics of its leadership and membership. In fact, there will never be a perfect church on this earth as long as there are people in it. Therefore, as believers and leaders we must determine to follow the counsel of God's Word to grow in the grace and knowledge of our Lord Jesus Christ.

If a leader has been too harsh in his style, he must ask God to change his disposition. Indeed, he may never satisfy everybody, but that is not the goal. The goal is to follow Jesus and to edify His people.

To avoid confusion, consider the difference between pleasing the congregation and edifying the congregation. **To please** people, make them happy or satisfied, fulfill their wishes and wills. **To edify** is to instruct so as to promote intellectual and moral improvement.

Suspicious, skeptical and, yes, hurting persons can react against leadership to the point that they begin to lose balance in and perspective on the Christian life. The suspicious and cynical person will reject nearly anything the parent, pastor or leader teaches him. Often a good principle is rejected merely because someone else used to say that. The person who has become cynical becomes the very thing he accused. The Bible states that "a false balance is abomination." [18]

When a person becomes reactionary rather than causative, he quickly loses balance. This is true of a pastor who reacts against some leader in his denomination or fellowship, or a pastor who reacts at people who have reacted against him! He who overreacts loses. We victimize ourselves when we respond to abuse negatively.

There can be no doubt that servant leaders today face two major challenges: First, we must appropriate God's grace in our own lives to ensure that past hurts will not claim current and future spiritual and leadership victories. It must be well with our souls if we will lead others into a closer walk with God. Second, we must help those in this hostile culture to know the love and forgiveness of God. While there will be those who choose to remain cynical and suspicious, there are many more who will appreciate our steadfast demonstration of Christian love and caring on their behalf.

We inhabit a difficult yet potential-filled period in the history of the church. We have opportunities, mediums and resources to reach a lost and dying world like never before. We also have a ministry of reconciliation to the hurting and suspicious. As spiritual leaders, our love for the Saviour must be intense, and our commitment to share His love and grace, equally strong. We must admit where we have been wrong and go on for the Lord, secure in the second chances He freely offers. So let us be encouraged and continue to go forward.

CHAPTER 5
Phoenix

"Conflict that hones the edge of an organization and
keeps it mindful of and true to its purposes is healthy." [1]

Charles H. Spurgeon—the name alone evokes a sense
of mystery and admiration from contemporary servant
leaders. His legacy seems unattainable; his testimony,
somewhat unearthly; however, he was just a man. He
was a man with a desire to honor God, honor His Word,
preach an undiluted Gospel and serve the flock
entrusted to him by a Saviour of grace increasing. Considered in this fashion, I can identify with a man who
contended for the Faith in his own generation.

Spurgeon's contentions focused upon baptismal
regeneration, Arminianism and liberalism in the Baptist
Union. "This controversy raged in the pages of religious
publications, with some writers even questioning Spurgeon's conversion! 'I am not easily put down,' Spurgeon
wrote to a friend. 'I go right on and care for no man on
God's earth.'" [2]

During a later battle, a friend questioned whether he
might not be "in hot water." "Oh, no," Spurgeon
replied. "It is the other fellows who are in hot water. I
am the stoker, the man who makes the water boil." [3]
These responses testify of a man whose character balanced him in distress as he defended the doctrines of

God's grace. However, this same man confessed, "I am the subject of depressions of spirit so fearful that I hope none of you ever get to such extremes of wretchedness as I go to."[4]

One author sympathizes with Spurgeon, saying:

> Few preachers have experienced the kind of criticism that Spurgeon did when he began his ministry in London. A steady stream of magazine articles and pamphlets examined the young preacher's character, words, works, and motives, and most of them were anything but sympathetic. More than one writer expressed doubts that Spurgeon was even converted! His sermons were called "trashy," and he was compared to a rocket that would climb high and then suddenly drop out of sight! "What is he doing?" one writer asked. "Whose servant is he? What proof does he give that, instrumentally, his is a heart-searching, a Christ-exalting, a truth-unfolding, a sinner-converting, a church-feeding, a soul-saving ministry?"[5]

> At first, this criticism deeply hurt Spurgeon, but then the Lord gave him peace and victory. Hearing slanderous reports of his character and ministry week after week could have led him into defeat; but he fell to his knees and prayed, "Master, I will not keep back even my character for Thee. If I must lose that, too, then let it go; it is the dearest thing I have, but it shall go, if, like my Master, they shall say I have a devil, and am mad, or, like Him, I am a drunken man and wine-bibber."[6]

A reminder: Grace is a disposition created within the heart of a man or woman yielded to the Holy Spirit of God. Spurgeon possessed this disposition and was "gentle unto all men, apt to teach, patient, In meekness instructing those that [opposed him]"[7] during a critical period. God's servants are equipped to channel their trials and pressures through the funnel of God's grace.

Grace enables a **response** that is kind toward the

unkind actions of others. Grace is a balm that prompts us to say in company with the psalmist, "It is good for me that I have been afflicted."[8] Our fleshly **reaction** is to scream, "No, it's not! It's not good at all, and you just don't know about this problem or that person or the person who is the problem." However, a grace-induced **response** compliments the psalmist who concluded that his affliction was **good** "that [he] might learn [His] statutes."[9]

Servant leaders are drawn to the Word, and our challenges drive us to it, which is a **good** result because there we discover Jesus who was "full of grace and truth."[10] His Word guarantees that servants will suffer persecution;[11] however, "God is able to make all grace abound toward [them in order that they], always having all sufficiency in all things, may abound to every good work."[12] God's final exhortation concerning the matter commands, "Preach the word; be instant in season, out of season; reprove, rebuke, exhort with all longsuffering and doctrine."[13] To which seasons is he referring? Solomon defined this for us when he instructed, "To every thing there is a season, and a time to every purpose under the heaven."[14] He acknowledges there is:

> "A time to kill, and a time to heal; a time to break down, and a time to build up; A time to weep, and a time to laugh; a time to mourn, and a time to dance; A time to cast away stones, and a time to gather stones together; a time to embrace, and a time to refrain from embracing; A time to get, and a time to lose; a time to keep, and a time to cast away; A time to rend, and a time to sew; a time to keep silence, and a time to speak; A time to love, and a time to hate; a time of war, and a time of peace."[15]

Might we use a little sanctified imagination by drawing an application? The killing, breaking down, weeping, mourning, casting stones, refraining from embraces, losing, casting away, rending, silencing, hating and warring characterize the critical periods of every servant leader's life and ministry. May we further assert that the healing, building up, laughing, dancing, gathering, embracing, getting, keeping, sewing, speaking, loving and peace-keeping are sure promises from a God "that cannot lie."[16] They are the fruitful seasons that follow the crises as long as our confidence remains in Christ. Degeneration into carnality produces rotten fruit, not planted nor intended by the Spirit of God who fertilizes our souls with grace. When this grace is manifest, our lives harvest a message greater than our own spoken words could possibly produce.

I have personally met and spoken with Christians who claim an uncanny, almost mystical understanding of grace. My part is to accept their testimony; however, I have witnessed these same people express feelings of bitterness, characterized by corrupt or angry communication. Does this render their claims invalid? No. It simply means that their humanity stalks their good intentions and can assume carnal forms. It is a worthy statement: A fixed distance separates the "grace talk" from the "grace walk." Someone on the "grace walk" will not play the blame game for long. And human, servant leaders are vulnerable to a ministry of mere talking if they will not yield their lives and ministries to the discipline of routine spiritual assessments with the intent of adjustment to a more grace-filled walk. They should appropriate God's grace and **keep moving forward.**

The day had finally ended. The sun had made its westward decline hours earlier. What response might have revealed the character of the day's events? "You would not believe the day I've had! One thing after another! Hardly time for a breather, let alone the rest and study I longed for!" Sound familiar? These hectic, pressure-filled days form the pattern for ministry. And they should, for the One after whom we model our ministries experienced them too, as recorded in the Gospel according to Mark. Jesus received news that His intimate friend John the Baptist had lost his head—literally! His immediate felt need was to depart into a desert place with His disciples to rest; however, that was not possible, for a large crowd followed Him into the wilderness. Despite His weariness, He performed a miracle feeding five thousand people. And just as He reached that coveted place apart in the mountain to pray, He discovered His disciples tossed by the wind and sea. His grief mingled with exhaustion did not impede His quick action to calm the sea and save His disciples from sure catastrophe.

Every fruitful Christian servant has an adventure to relate. The details may differ, but the experience is the same. Our church or organization is calmly accomplishing its mission only to be interrupted without warning by turbulence: someone is hurt physically or offended emotionally, and our response—not reaction—is expected.

One report reveals the alarming rate at which pastors and missionaries are quitting the ministry. An extensive survey of men shepherding works of 75 to 200 people disclosed these results:[17]

1. Ninety percent of pastors work in excess of 46 hours weekly;

2. Eighty percent believe that the ministry adversely affects their families;

3. Seventy-five percent reported significant stress-related illnesses (in 1991, the Southern Baptist Convention spent 64 million dollars on health insurance to cover medical costs pertaining to stress-related illnesses among their pastors);

4. Seventy percent of the pastors had a lower self-esteem after several years in the ministry, trying to serve God's people;

5. Seventy percent said they felt as though they had no close friend;

6. Eighty-one percent said they had insufficient time with their wives.

The contemporary minister must exercise a particular fruit of the Spirit with regard to these facts: it is called long-suffering. True long-suffering:

> bears quite happily everything that is done against it, resents not at all being trampled underfoot, and reacts to the wrongdoing of others against itself as though no wrong had been done at all, or else as though it had forgotten all about it! For long-suffering is really the lovely quality of forgiveness and bearing contentedly and joyfully the results of the mistakes and wrongdoing of others.[18]

This is not a human quality: it is a Christlike quality—the quality of a Christian. Our conflicts are necessary, for they afford us the opportunity to appropriate God's grace. Not all disagreements among Christians are unhealthy or hurtful. At times we will discover that our most precious dreams, goals and visions are sacrificed on the altar of a fiery trial, and we are left with only the ashes of our memory.

The ancient myth of the **Phoenix** reveals a bird, unusual in the glory of its appearance, which was thought to be the servant of a god. The myth says that this bird rejoiced daily with a song so powerful and affectionate in its performance that its god would stop his chariot each morning to hear the winsome melody. This lovely bird was destroyed in fire, but from its ashes it arose more splendidly beautiful than it had been or could have been if not for the testing fire.

Similarly, today's servants of the living and true God can arise from the ashes renewed, restored and ready to serve our Saviour and Lord more beautifully—the Saviour who identified Himself with sinners that they may become servants who could identify with Him. The Son of God was made the Son of Man—

> crucified by the sin of men, bearing it all, feeling it all and overcoming it all, that by so doing He might be able to overcome the disease of sin in the whole suffering body or race of men. Think of what it means to be able to save and to heal—to be able to raise up out of that which has been so cruelly marred and diseased, something far more glorious than would otherwise have been possible.[19]

Sometimes we must allow and patiently endure those things that we have never wanted in order to achieve those things that we have always wanted. One's character is not *developed* in the crisis; it is *revealed*.

Have you ever shared a dream and been disbelieved or, worse, mocked even by those you assumed would share your joy and love you most? Have you ever had a brother turn on you and leave? When you sensed the Lord was with you, that restoration would become reality, have you instead found yourself in a prison of consequences that you did not invite? Or maybe you were forgotten when you deserved to be remembered. Have you forgiven those who disbelieved, turned against, left, imprisoned or forgot you?

One man did, and his name was Joseph. He was sold into slavery by his brothers, degenerated beyond measure by his own flesh and blood—yet he loved them. He graciously spared their lives when unknowingly they sought sustenance at his hand. His life is our example of responding in grace to the injustices of life. We also must respond in grace to adversity, and this can be accomplished in practical ways if we will submit to the disciplines of the Christian life.

A critic is a person whose spiritual wounds have never been allowed to heal. The problem is a spiritual one although it may like a cancer attack other social organs, affecting the critic's emotional, mental and physical well-being. Like the cancer patient, he must be diagnosed carefully and treated with great care.

We must not rush to call one who disagrees with us a critic; however, when a genuine critical spirit is threatening the ministry, remain faithful to the Word that God has entrusted to you and pray for your enemies. **Above all else, pray.** A Christian cliché notes that "prayer changes things"; however, prayer changes people too! If our prayers seem powerless to alter the critic's viewpoint, perhaps they will alter ours.

The greatest single need of the servant of God is time with God in prayer. Our battles are won in our prayer closets. David begged, "Plead my cause, O LORD, with them that strive with me: fight against them that fight against me." [20] We cannot strive with the critic, but God can. He wrestled Jacob and blinded Paul. He can awaken the conscience and change the heart of your adversary too.

Sometimes we act like we are surprised when the term "sovereignty" comes up in a conversation in relation to our conflicts. We don't say it, but we act like it: *Oh, right—I almost forgot that You are God.* What is the cause of this unfortunate case of spiritual amnesia?

I think it is that we do not live in the assurance of God's love. We live in the security and assurance of our salvation but not always of His love. We may not question Him verbally, but we do question Him inwardly, and as a result our spiritual life deteriorates. Why? It is because we were created and saved to experience the reality of intimacy, the experience of a love relationship, with our Lord.

Proverbs 3:32 confides, "For the froward is abomination to the LORD: but **his secret** is with the righteous." A footnote in the Ryrie Study Bible provides this comment—"perverse individuals are an abomination to God, but He deals with the righteous as **His intimate friends.**"

God loves us, and God will never express Himself in any other way but love toward us. Each of us must determine in his own heart to view his circumstances always against the backdrop of the cross. "We love him, because he first loved us,"[21] even in adversity. Receive these present difficulties as a friend to develop you. Rest in His love. Rest in this circumstance that God has allowed for your benefit. We must rest in His sovereignty.

A lack of recognition of God's sovereignty leads to overreaction. To illustrate, leaders become disappointed with the actions of mentors. We are human, and disappointment is a part of our humanity—a given in a fallen world. But in their further reaction, they abandon the Biblical truths and practices of mentors. This behavior produces the result opposite of their intention; for in their attempt to escape the influence of their previous guides, their unresolved bitterness toward them dictates their lives and ministries. This resembles the false concept of peer pressure. Pressure may exist among peers, but once a person submits to that pressure, it is no longer among peers: the one who submits lowers himself to the will of the person exerting the pressure.

Ministers can also react to the conduct or misconduct of the flock or community. They cease to lift up Jesus Christ in their own hearts and before the people God has called them to serve.

A few years ago, I learned through a personal crisis the importance of focusing on Jesus rather than others or myself. Realizing the need for God-centered living, I established a theme for my life and for our church in the upcoming year. The theme was "Look to Jesus." I have found that the wounds we suffer in ministry will heal if we don't pick at them. We must allow the healing ointment of God's grace to cover our weaknesses and heal our disappointments.

If grace can be analogous to ointment, then forgiveness

is the Band-Aid; it covers a multitude of transgressions. As leaders, we must acknowledge the differences in spiritual maturity or lack thereof in those whom God has placed "in our house." It is our responsibility to cultivate an atmosphere of forgiveness which enhances the opportunities for spiritual maturity to take place in the lives of believers.

Forgiveness can be illustrated using two familiar passages of Scripture. Ephesians 4:30–32 admonishes,

"And grieve not the holy Spirit of God, whereby ye are sealed unto the day of redemption. Let all bitterness, and wrath, and anger, and clamour, and evil speaking, be put away from you, with all malice: And be ye kind one to another, tenderhearted, forgiving one another, even as God for Christ's sake hath forgiven you."

Notice again the phrase, **"forgiving one another, even as God for Christ's sake hath forgiven you."** Personal application of this command requires an understanding of how it is that Christ has forgiven us; for in the same way He forgave us, we are to forgive others.

Flip back a few books to Romans 5:8 and recall that "while we were yet sinners, Christ died for us." Our humanness practically forces us to neglect the counsel of this instruction. We think the person who is hurting us must stop doing that annoying or abusive thing before we can forgive him. But God set the example: even while we were still sinning, even while we were still abusing the principle of love and grieving the Holy Spirit—He forgave us in Christ. And in Christ, we can forgive those who do not notice or do not care about the effects of their mistreatment of us.

* * *

A traveler was making his way with a guide through the jungles of Burma. They came to a shallow but wide river and waded through it to the other side. When the traveler came out of the river, numerous leeches had attached to his torso and legs. His first instinct was to grab them and pull them off.

His guide stopped him, warning that pulling the leeches off would only leave tiny pieces of them under the skin. Eventually, infection would set in.

The best way to rid the body of the leeches, the guide advised, was to bathe in a warm balsam bath for several minutes. This would soak the leeches, and soon they would release their hold on the man's body.

* * *

When another person significantly injures me, I cannot simply yank the injury from myself and expect that all bitterness, malice and emotion will be gone. Resentment still hides under the surface. The only way to become truly free of the offense and to forgive others is to bathe in the soothing bath of God's forgiveness. When I finally fathom the extent of God's love in Jesus Christ, forgiveness of others is a natural outflow.

The Bible says in Proverbs 11:14, "Where no counsel is, the people fall: but in the multitude of counsellors there is safety." If there is ever a time to seek godly counsel, it is during times of severe trial and criticism. We must increase our accountability and accessibility to trusted friends and advisors who will pray with and for us. Stressed-out Christians usually make really bad choices. We should "surround [ourselves] with spiritual advisors, men of godly wisdom....The counsel and consent of mature advisors will steady [our] hand amidst the bombardment."[22]

Some years ago, during a time of particular blessing and growth in our church, I received a newsletter from a church on the East Coast. This newsletter had been mailed to several thousand pastors across America. It lacked a Christ-centered philosophy, and its tone was caustic. The editors had constructed a rambling analysis of various Baptist churches. My name and the names of several other pastors were labeled with the word "compromise" because we did not espouse the exact methods or employ the same special speakers as the editors' churches.

Of course there was an initial desire to defend the integrity of our ministry by responding to this man. However, I thank God for a few praying friends whose help caused me to keep those really insignificant issues in perspective and keep on with the main work of winning souls for Christ. As my grandmother once told me, "One reason a dog has so many friends is that he wags his tail, not his tongue."

When we are hurt, we often feel like retreating into a secluded world where we can heal and be restored. It's like having the flu. We want someone to bring us hot, homemade chicken soup with soda water or juice, saltine crackers, a warm blanket and gobs of sympathy. Our times of adversity can be likened to a spiritual flu—instead of losing control over our bodies, we feel like we've lost control over the very circumstances that plague us. Therefore, it is important to care for ourselves just as if we were sick.

This does not require that we purchase "positive thinking" tapes or repeat words of affirmation to ourselves in the mirror. Three ways of taking care of ourselves spiritually are to humble ourselves before God, to continue growing in grace and to love our families.

Humility before God promises more grace; for the Word says, "But he giveth more grace. Wherefore he saith, God resisteth the proud, but giveth grace unto the humble." [23] **Growth in grace** promises God's sufficiency for continued ministry. The Word confirms this, promising that "God is able to make all grace abound toward you; that ye, always having all sufficiency in all things, may abound to every good work." [24] And finally, **loving our families** recruits a home team rooting for us, loving us and standing by us during our crisis of belief.

Never was this more eloquently stated than by Ruth in the Old Testament when she said to Naomi, "Intreat me not to leave thee, or to return from following after thee: for whither thou goest, I will go; and where thou lodgest, I will lodge: thy people shall be my people, and thy God my God: Where thou diest, will I die, and there will I be buried: the Lord do so to me, and more also, if ought but death part thee and me."[25]

So after we pray and choose not to retaliate, then we should forgive, seek godly counsel, grow in grace, humble ourselves, love our families and fix our eyes upon Jesus, **remembering our calling.** We do not need to tangle with the critics when we can teach the children. Paul directed Timothy to commit to faithful men the things he had heard—men who would be able to teach others also. We may feel like we're not achieving much during a critical time, but **encouragement is an accomplishment.** Whenever we invest our lives in others, we are succeeding in the calling God has given us.

Mark it down—ministry goes on. If we quit, then the choice was ours. The **response** is ours. We shouldn't allow a person to steal God's best for us, allow one critic to capitalize on our insecurities, conclude our ministries because of one bad forecast, doubt God's strength because of our weakness. Don't quit. God is always at work around us in order that we, our families, our churches and even the critics might be conformed to the image of His dear Son, Jesus Christ. We should allow Him to have His perfect work in and around us, waiting upon Him as He turns our ashes into something beautiful. We must rise up from those ashes, dust ourselves off and continue our song and our ministry in order that we may please the One who has called us and confirmed His love to us time and again.

The Gospel Commandments of Leadership

Author unknown

1. **People are illogical, unreasonable and self-centered. Love and trust them anyway.** "Then said Jesus, Father, forgive them; for they know not what they do" (Luke 23:34).

2. **If you do good, people will accuse you of selfish, ulterior motives. Do good anyway.** "But whereunto shall I liken this generation? It is like unto children." "The Son of man came eating and drinking, and they say, Behold a man gluttonous, and a winebibber, a friend of publicans and sinners. But wisdom is justified of her children" (Matt. 11:16, 19).

3. **If you are successful, you will win false friends and true enemies. Succeed anyway.** The crowds who cheered Him on Sunday and called Him King were the same who cried, "Crucify Him!" "And as he went, they spread their clothes in the way. And when he was come nigh, even now at the descent of the mount of Olives...Saying, Blessed be the King that cometh in the name of the Lord: peace in heaven, and glory in the highest" (Luke 19:36–38).

"But they cried out, Away with him, away with him, crucify him" (John 19:15).

4. **The service you render today will be forgotten tomorrow. Serve people anyway.** "And Jesus answering said, Were there not ten cleansed? but where are the nine?" (Luke 17:17).

5. **Honesty and frankness will make you vulnerable. Be honest and frank anyway.** "Suppose ye that I am come to give peace on earth? I tell you, Nay; but rather division" (Luke 12:51).

"I tell you, Nay: but, except ye repent, ye shall all likewise perish" (Luke 13:5).

6. **The biggest men with the biggest ideas can be**

shot down by the smallest men with the smallest ideas. Think big anyway. "And truly the Son of man goeth, as it was determined." "And there was also a strife among them, which of them should be accounted the greatest" (Luke 22:22, 24).

7. People pretend to love the "little" people but sell their souls to the "big" people. Fight for the "little" people anyway. "But Jesus said, Suffer little children, and forbid them not, to come unto me: for of such is the kingdom of heaven" (Matt. 19:14).

8. What you spend years building may be destroyed overnight. Build anyway. "Now he that betrayed him gave them a sign, saying, Whomsoever I shall kiss, that same is he: hold him fast. And forthwith he came to Jesus, and said, Hail, master; and kissed him." "But all this was done, that the scriptures of the prophets might be fulfilled. Then all the disciples forsook him, and fled" (Matt. 26:48, 49, 56).

9. People really need help but may attack you if you do help. Help people anyway. "The Spirit of the Lord is upon me, because he hath anointed me to preach the gospel to the poor; he hath sent me to heal the brokenhearted, to preach deliverance to the captives, and recovering of sight to the blind, to set at liberty them that are bruised, To preach the acceptable year of the Lord." "And all they in the synagogue, when they heard these things, were filled with wrath, And rose up, and thrust him out of the city, and led him unto the brow of the hill whereon their city was built, that they might cast him down headlong" (Luke 4:18, 19, 28, 29).

10. Give the world the best you have, and you'll get kicked in the teeth. Give the world the best you have anyway. "Therefore when they were gathered together, Pilate said unto them, Whom will ye that I release unto you? Barabbas, or Jesus which is called Christ?" "They said, Barabbas" (Matt. 27:17, 21).

CHAPTER 6

Winds of Change

"Men have discovered that leading a church is extremely tough...when values are vanishing, social mores are shifting, and families are falling apart." [1]

Critical periods are common to the ministry experience. Conflict produces a crisis of belief for the servant leader. We cannot stay where we are and go with God. We must adjust and experience God through obedience or remain unchanged, refusing to be conformed to the image of Christ.

How is it that we affirm Biblical truth concerning the conforming and renewing work of the Spirit within us but don't consider that such changes will become evident in our motivation, method and ministry? It astonishes me how often we will admit that change is necessary in our lives, but we will not effectuate the change. I have heard dozens of pastors admit, "I need to improve my organizational skills," or "I love my family, but I just don't spend enough time with them—I'm winning my community and losing my own family." The transparency of such confessions evokes sympathy, but the sincere regret expressed rarely produces a sincere effort or change to remedy the situation.

God's ammunition against this form of spiritual apathy is adversity. He allows the pressure of ministry to strip away our pride and our complacency until we are prepared for the next level of ministry.

Grace is the author of vision: we see, within the context of our relationship with God, the opportunity to accomplish a work for His glory that exceeds our own ability. We often sing of grace; however, we become most sensitive to the reality of grace in our weakness. The adventures of the Apostle Paul almost play out like an action-hero saga. However, between shipwrecks, snake-bites and synagogue appearances, he testified "that the things which happened unto [him had] fallen out rather unto the furtherance of the gospel."[2]

The God of the past is the same today and forever-more; and just as Paul's crises made him a candidate for increased sufficiency and strength by grace and resulted in the furtherance of his ministry, so we are afforded the same opportunity in our adversity. God uses trials to produce **needed change.** This change is the result of a midcourse adjustment, an agent of blessing. The blessing is born of a Spirit-initiated paradigm shift to communicate a new view of the Lord and a new view of the capacity the ministry has to reach the community and the world for Christ.

"And I said, Oh that I had wings like a dove! for then would I fly away, and be at rest."—Ps. 55:6.

Following the completion of our first major building program, the Lord increased our church by several hundred new members per year for a number of years. Just prior to those showers of grace, I encountered one of the greatest seasons of conflict and difficulty in my life.

As a young pastor, I desired to do a great work for God. I wanted to walk close to God. Unfortunately, however, I also wanted a few of my early ministry mentors to take note of my progress in the ministry. These desires competed in my life because regardless of how one rationalizes, it is impossible to please both God and men. My efforts were rewarded by the praise of men in the form of my mentors' taking notice of my ministry. From them I derived a sense of false and misleading significance. However, the church was growing, and so I was happy, and my mentors were impressed—all was well, but not with my soul. I had allowed my focus to shift away from my Lord. Because of His great love and jealousy over His children, God allowed crises in my life that would empty me of my resources and my agenda and cause me to seek Him alone.

It was during this trial that a man who had mentored and influenced me greater than any other (excepting my Lord and my wife) failed in his ministry, which led to his resignation from a well-known pulpit. The choices he had made produced devastating effects upon many people. The shock and betrayal which I felt attacked my innermost being. For weeks I cried myself to sleep. On many Sundays I wondered how I could continue preaching. I began to fear the ministry, and on a few occasions Satan tempted me to quit the ministry or at least change my affiliations and position.

Slowly but steadfastly God's amazing grace began its healing and instructing work in my mind and in my heart. God was changing me or, should I say, shifting my focus away from men and to Him regardless of my circumstances. The psalmist recorded,

"Hear, O LORD, when I cry with my voice: have mercy also upon me, and answer me. When thou saidst, Seek ye my face; my heart said unto thee, Thy face, LORD, will I seek. Hide not thy face far from me; put not thy servant away in anger: thou hast been my help; leave me not, neither forsake me, O God of my salvation."[3]

Thankfully, I did not forsake my calling or my doctrinal position, which is a real temptation to many that face similar circumstances and are disappointed by a dominant mentor. I searched the Scripture anew and realized that God had not forsaken me; in fact, in my grief and doubt, He gathered me up as His child. I could not forsake my doctrinal position because of the failures of men, even men I loved and respected.

Several years after our first building program was completed, the growth of our ministry necessitated the construction of a new auditorium. Any pastor who has built so much as an outhouse can testify that building programs are often accompanied by spiritual warfare, and the first target within enemy sites is usually the pastor. Just prior to the construction of that new auditorium, I was visited by yet another season of great challenge; this time the battle raged within me. While my previous conflict had been caused by actions outside of me through the failure of a mentor, this new challenge rose up inside of me in the form of idolatry which had crept into my heart. I know that I am not the only pastor who is susceptible to this idol that is called the church. It seems so natural to love and worship the ministry and give more to it than to God Himself.

With reflection, I believe that God used that challenge to readjust my focus to Him in preparation for a new assignment, which required greater responsibility. He lovingly allowed winds of change to blow again. Through a series of misunderstandings and disappointments, God created a season in my life whereby He could first work *in* me before He could work *through* me.

I have observed that every maturing Christian encounters trials and is called to navigate through rough seas and winds of change; however, not every Christian allows the Spirit of God to change his heart in these times of changed circumstance. He has charted his course, and not even God's Spirit can redirect or refocus it. The sooner a leader follows His leading, the more prepared he will be for His blessings. There is purpose in the struggle, and it is God's purpose. In the struggle we seek Him and adjust to Him, and our ministries are improved by the changes that result.

These inward conflicts and crises of belief pained me; however, I am now convinced that God desired to **work in me,** BEFORE **working through me** in the days that would follow the completion of the building project. I needed adjustment. God initiated that adjustment with pressure, pressure which prompted change.

Change is a courageous endeavor, and courage is an affair of the heart. This courage is measured to us by the Lord at appropriate times and is usually manifest when we hurt enough to change, when we learn enough to want to change, and finally, when we receive enough that we must change. God initiates change primarily among individuals, but He uses those individuals to change His church.

My struggles preceding the completion of our building project were personal; however, sometimes God guides an entire congregation into a critical period for the purpose of adjustment and renewal.

"And straightway the father of the child cried out, and said with tears, Lord, I believe; help thou mine unbelief."—Mark 9:24.

Some years ago, I was enjoying lunch with pastor friends in Los Angeles. One of these men, a trusted friend and advisor, spoke candidly about ministry challenges, changes. We cleaned our plates and dispersed our fellowship. I got into my car and started speeding down Interstate 14 due north. My cell phone rang. On the other end was a fearful voice. A staff member rehashed the terrible news. Three of our young ladies from the college had been struck by a passing semi-truck while turning out of the church parking lot. The tragedy occurred while our grade-schoolers were being let out of classes. Hundreds of children and also adults had witnessed the horrific scene. Stunned crowds gathered around the wreckage. Ambulances and helicopters transported the injured. One of them was Jessica Downey. She was not breathing, was not expected to live.

I felt numb. I replaced the phone and began to weep and to pray that God might spare her life. The Downey family was a "first family." They had stood by us and joined with us when our family had first come to Lancaster, when all we had were suitcases and a dream. My wife had led Jessica to Christ. I had led her father, John, to Christ.

I remember the hospital, the emergency room. John was on his knees near the door. Jessica lay inside—silent, still. We waited. The attending physician appeared and advised, "I do not believe Jessica will survive the brain and heart damage she has sustained in the accident. I would like to recommend that you consider donating her remaining organs to help perhaps save someone else's life."

During the passing hours, a miracle occurred, and it wasn't Jessica's recovery. Hundreds of people from our church and college began pouring into the hospital, not to visit but to pray. The doctor returned and repeated his previous warning, adding that she would not make it through the night.

The sun rose in the east, and still many were on their knees. Jessica was comatose. Days, weeks and months passed. Jessica lay still. Hundreds continued the prayer vigil. In the Sunday edition of our local paper, a front-page story asked, "Who is Jessica, and who are these people?"

The focus of our church family was riveted on Jessica. Her trauma occupied center stage. But God was accomplishing a unifying work among us behind the scenes. The plot of His choosing was unfolding. Families were sharing, children were praying, teenagers and parents were bonding, college students were interceding—a result that no organized church meeting or revival meeting could provide.

One morning around 2:00 a.m., following a pro-longed season of prayer with men from our church, I turned a corner. I found a place on the hallway floor and considered the events surrounding me. What possible good thing or things could God be teaching me at such a terrible time? Several things entered my mind:

1. Because of the trial and the subsequent days of prayer, my heart was more open to God's teaching and direction than ever before in my life.

2. Prayer was more real and more spontaneous than at any other time in my life.

3. Opportunities to witness were everywhere, and many people were making decisions to accept Christ as Saviour.

4. There was a refining work underway in my heart and in the hearts of our church family.

5. A new humility possessed my conscience.

6. I experienced God intimately.

7. God was being approached, praised, honored, wor-shiped and glorified more readily.

Several weeks later with family and friends around her bedside, God woke Jessica from the coma; and through many challenging months of therapy and rehabilitation Jessica has been able to return to her fam-ily, to her college and to her church family. At nearly every service Jessica sits on my left in the second row of the church, and her presence there is a constant reminder to me and our church family of the lessons and adjustments God allowed for our benefit in 1997.

In acceptance lieth peace,
  O my heart be still;
Let thy restless worries cease
  And accept His will.
Though this test be not thy choice,
It is His—therefore rejoice.

In His plan there cannot be
   Aught to make thee sad:
If this is His choice for thee,
   Take it and be glad.
Make from it some lovely thing
To the glory of thy King.

Cease from sighs and murmuring,
   Sing His loving grace.
This thing means thy furthering
   To a wealthy place.
From thy fears He'll give release,
In acceptance lieth peace.[4]

Through the trials, hurts and disappointments of life God is still at work. Suffering qualifies us for ministry more than any class or course offered. Christian character does not come via Federal Express. In a world that is intoxicated with meeting schedules and success stories, God is inviting us to slow down, "take [His] yoke upon [us,] and learn of [Him.]"[5]

> Sometimes I went so far as to thank destiny for the privilege of such loneliness, for only in solitude could I have scrutinized my past so carefully or examined so closely my interior and outward life. What strong and strange new germs of hope were born in my soul during those memorable hours! I weighed and decided all sorts of issues; I entered into a compact with myself to avoid the errors of former years and the rocks on which I had been wrecked.[6]

We must allow the inner prompting of the Spirit to guide us into necessary spiritual adjustment that we may be equipped and made adequate for the future ministry He has planned. Unfortunately, many of us don't experience this because we didn't pencil it into our Day-Timers. And when God does initiate the process, we focus on causes and consequences instead of purposes. When a person suffers, others are prone to look to the past to find a reason for the trial—a connection between prior sin and present suffering.

In contrast, the Bible often notes a connection between present suffering and future glory. The purpose of suffering is seen, not in its cause but in its results. It seems as if Jessica endured adversity so that our church family might vicariously experience the perfecting and renewing work of God. I can hardly appreciate enough Jessica's acceptance, with joy, of her circumstances. God entrusted to her a large assignment—the renewing of our church body.

God is always at work in our lives, even in conflict. So often we read about heroes of the Faith and marvel at the big assignments they received from God and accomplished for His glory. But we don't often see the pain, the struggle and even the loss they endured. We must keep in mind that while the Bible is full of the big assignments God entrusted to His servants, volumes could be filled with the unpublished details of little assignments—assignments that prepared servants for a task God had ordained. The ministries for which God's servants volunteered required them to submit to the special challenges that accompany Christian service.

For example, Amy Carmichael is a twentieth-century hero of the Faith. Although it took her almost a decade (full of little assignments) to "find herself" on the mission field, she quickly made up for lost time and attacked the large assignments with fervor and faith as an advocate for temple children in Hindu India. Her extensive work was centered in sound evangelism and social ministry; however, she was challenged greatly by pressures from the Hindu nationals, dissension among workers, criticism from outsiders and, finally, physical trauma. A serious fall incurring internal injuries and a badly broken foot placed Amy on her bed where she was confined until her death.

While on her bed, **by faith** Amy produced a small library of autobiographical literature that has inspired and chastened each succeeding generation of Christians. "By it [she] being dead yet speaketh."[7]

> Accept for yourself the Fatherhood of God, which is only possible for you and me because of the sacrifice of the blessed Son, our Saviour. **And by the presence of the Holy Spirit within, you will learn to rejoice in the Word of God, and nothing else.** This, then, is the call to the soul that would ascend above all earthly circumstance, to walk in heavenly places: leave yourself open to the circumstances of His choice, for that is perfect acceptance. Rest in the Word of God.[8]

We cannot foresee what God has ordained for our today or tomorrow, but we can let the adversity we experience have its perfecting work in our lives. More than that, we can take our cue and assess our personal lives and ministries, allowing God to initiate needed change. Let us pray to be established rather than beg for the escape. Dare we excuse ourselves from the blessings which are hidden for only a season?

Another avenue of God's choosing, which is designed to prompt spiritual evaluation and adjustment, is the counsel of godly friends that we might gain spiritual perspective. God entrusted a special friend of mine in the ministry to write the following letter to me at a crucial time. Parts of it have been reproduced below with my friend's permission. I trust it will minister to your heart just as it ministered to mine.

Pastor,

> When a man is greatly used of God, his life always comes to those moments where some very critical reassessments have to be made. It is how we respond to these periods of reevaluation that can indeed make all of the difference in the world as to how the Lord leads in the waiting periods of our lives.

These seasons of measurement are brought on by the loving ministry of the Holy Spirit who is endeavoring to get us to make the periodic mid-course changes that are so vital to the successful completion of our course. The tool of emotion, which the Holy Spirit often uses during these times, is a feeling of a need for reassurance in our spirit, or a sense of detached dissatisfaction. This is done to capture our attention and to prepare us for the needed change. The man who surprisingly "works through" these periods when the Holy Spirit is endeavoring to get him to change is engaged in a perilous pursuit. He is placing in position in the course of his life the signpost which reads, "I will not change" and "I will not yield." In time, the Holy Spirit will withdraw His prompting from this man. He will proceed with his ministry exactly as he was before, feeling quite sure that what he experienced was nothing more than a simple emotional upset or, at worst, some notice of a humanly manufactured midlife or career crisis. But having "weathered it" and "gotten over it," he is ready to go on for the Lord, little realizing the frustration to the leading of God he has brought about in his life.

There are moments in the life of every Christian when through fatigue, illness or other frustrating circumstances we can feel a sense of despair or an element of dissatisfaction. But that is normally distinguishably different from when the Spirit of God moves with His prompting to prepare us for even greater usefulness for the cause of Christ. When the emotions we are experiencing are due to fatigue and matters of that nature, there is almost always a recognition certain within our hearts of what the problem is and what we can do to correct it.

But when the Holy Spirit is moving upon us to disquiet our emotions and spirit for the reason of causing a change in our lives, we find ourselves more often baffled as to why we would feel the way that we are. Our reasoning says, "How, when the Lord is so blessing and perpetuating what we are venturing for Him, could I feel as I do?" In fact, we feel a sense of guilt at times as to how we could feel like this amidst all that the Lord is accomplishing.

The key in these moments of life is to seize upon all that the Lord is causing us to experience. We must not grieve or defeat the work of God's leading, but we should recognize the discomfort in our hearts as His schooling in us. To simply wait out His pull upon our heart is a tragedy recorded repeatedly in Scripture; however, when our spirit responds to the impulse of His leading, God is able to use us in greater measure.

Some would teach and preach that we are not to feel these moments of disquiet within our spirit (as they say that they never do), but I do not feel that to be the position of the Scriptures. David, so greatly used of God, bares his emotions and state of mind in the Psalms for all to read. The Bible is our almost continuous record of men and women whom the Lord used and changed when they stayed sensitive to His moving upon their spirit and emotion.

Greatness *for* God requires greatness *with* God. And that is where the acute sensitivity and a right reading of what the Lord is leading us to when He begins these moments of uneasiness in our hearts, are so vital. These seasons in our spirit are no accident or oversight with God. Rather, they are His midcourse graduate school for great usefulness.

You and you alone, Pastor, have to discern what the Lord is saying in these attentive, capturing moments with Him. Each message from God to His servant is virtually personal, and I would always be cautious when someone else endeavors to bring upon you his understanding of what the Lord wants in your life or ministry. For, outside of the Lord's expressed will in His Word, the Lord's leading and message to each is not for another to interpret or redirect.

So I am offering all that I am saying in order to encourage you to be a great Christian, a great pastor and preacher, and a loving and exemplary husband and father. But with all of the demands being made upon your time I feel that it is possible that the Lord is raising a moment of disquiet in your heart because the ever-expanding role the ministry is playing is totally capturing your time. Because the ministry is so worthy and of such honor to the Lord, we can easily justify giving it all of our time and priority of attention. But the man of God has to guard his own walk with the Lord and his time with his family above this. He has to capture his schedule before his schedule captures him.

There are some good men who need to have a fire built under them when it comes to working harder. But working hard at the expense of not giving the Lord and one's family a scheduled priority can be as disastrous in consequence as not working hard at all. The key for any pastor is that he learns to control his schedule, disallowing his schedule to control him.

Adjustment is an opportunity for a personal tutoring session with Jesus Himself. His instrument of instruction is ministry and life pressures. This learning process was important for every Biblical personality from Moses to the Apostle Paul. Adjustment can be defined in steps:

1. To make accurate by means of **evaluation** (observation);
2. To bring into **correct relationship** (God-ward);
3. To conform or **adjust** (the paradigm shift/inward change);
4. To **settle** a claim or debt (people-ward/outward change).

This process cannot be initiated without being completed. The result of the process is not determined by the performance of individual steps but by the completion of the cycle and the adoption of the process as a spiritual life discipline. *Evaluation* and *adjustment* are the words that define the assessment process. By God's grace we can evaluate the need for change and respond to that knowledge positively by making **needed adjustments.** In reality, the highest reward for a person's toil is not what he *gets* but what he *becomes.*

These adjustments begin with inward change as our intimacy with God is restored. This renewed fellowship becomes the canvas upon which God creates a new disposition, a paradigm shift applied with grace. These God-ward and inward changes are manifest outwardly, causing evident adjustment and decisive action as we seek to restore our relationships with family, friends, peers and the church with humility, forgiveness and grace. Learning is a change of behavior. We haven't truly learned anything until we act upon knowledge acquired in a decisive manner.

We were designed for intimacy with Christ, and we must be seeking time to establish this closeness. If we will acquire the needed grace to adjust, we must both schedule and then show up for our time with Him. "It is enough for the disciple to be as his Lord, and to learn also....There is absolutely no experience...which you can meet in the course of your earthly life, that can harm you if you will but let [Him] teach you how to accept it with joy."[9]

This instruction requires time in His presence. Consider the Biblical example of Mary of Bethany and her penchant for feet. She sat at the feet of Jesus to learn.[10] She fell at the feet of Jesus to weep.[11] She served at the feet of Jesus to worship.[12] **Every time** we see Mary she is at the feet of Jesus. You also must **take**

time to sit, weep and worship before Him.

Ministry like a whirlwind absorbs everything in its path until they are one—still moving but **forever intertwined**. Our families are caught up in this ministry whirlwind, and they also are consumed. Pastors may forsake their families for their ministries, but this is unnecessary. Our families are one with our ministries, and time must be allotted to their nurture and development as much or more so than to that of any other program or person in the church.

I have sensed the Holy Spirit convicting me about my personal need to enjoy my family, recognizing them as His supreme gift to me. Just a few hours ago as this day began, I had the privilege of reading Scripture and praying with my family. We discussed some fairly discouraging results from a recent California election; and as we prepared to load up the car and head for school, our youngest son, Matthew, piped up, "Remember Ephesians 6, Dad!" What a blessing to be reminded about God's spiritual armor by one of my kids!

The primary ministry of any pastor or Christian is his home. Remember Barnabas?[13] At a crucial moment, he chose to focus his primary ministry upon John Mark, his nephew. His secondary ministry did not cease, for the Bible indicates that Barnabas took Mark and sailed to Cyprus. Ryrie comments that "Barnabas' continued interest in John Mark rescued him from possible uselessness." Barnabas' commitment to his family bore fruit, because later Paul wrote to Timothy: "Do thy diligence to come shortly unto me"; "Take Mark, and bring him with thee: for he is profitable to me for the ministry."[14]

Every pastor desires that his family presently, and specifically his children in the future, will be found profitable in the ministry of God's leading. We must heed Barnabas' example and invest ourselves in our families. The fruit will follow.

Every pastor confesses that he has a heart for God. However, the strangest battle exists—a tendency for servants of God to substitute their **heart for God** with a **heart for ministry.** One lesson that the Lord has revealed to me during my periods of assessment is the *lesson of priorities.* He does not want my passion for ministry to supersede my passion for Him! A fine line exists, and every spiritual leader crosses it from time to time. God employs trials to indicate His desire for our heart first and our service second.

Observe Martha of Bethany.[15] She received Jesus into her home and, not unlike many of us, was cumbered about with much serving. Learn from this illustration: Martha is in the kitchen *serving.* Mary is in the sanctuary (sitting room) *worshiping.* On this particular occasion, Martha complains concerning her sister's *inactivity* but is lovingly rebuked by our Lord. He said kindly, "Martha, Martha, thou art careful and troubled about many things: But one thing is *needful."* **Martha needed change**, and the Lord Himself initiated that change.

Later, on a separate occasion, we meet these two extraordinary women again. Picture this:[16] Martha is in the kitchen *serving.* Mary is on the floor applying ointment to the feet of Jesus. The Bible testifies that **"some...had *indignation* within themselves, and said, Why was this waste of the ointment made?"** But Martha was not among those who complained. She was still serving, but her heart had been changed—turned from choleric to patient, from ingratitude to thankfulness; her attitude, from bitter to blessed. No longer would she allow her service to eclipse her worship.

While each of us can potentially take things into our own hands, wise is the spiritual leader who learns to loosen the grip and remembers to yield to Christ, who is the true Lord of ministry and the entire universe. Imagine the Prophet Jeremiah.[17] It's 597 B.C., and Assyrian

King Nebuchadnezzar captures Jerusalem and sets up Zedekiah as a puppet king. Threats abound that he will return to occupy the city. In the interim, Zedekiah imprisons Jeremiah for proclaiming the Word of the Lord. Amidst all this difficulty, God instructs Jeremiah to purchase a field offered by his cousin. In view of the advancing armies of Babylon, Jeremiah doubts the wisdom of securing land that will soon belong to a heathen king. God confirms His Word to Jeremiah, revealing the purpose for the purchase: Israel had turned from God, and God was now turning the Chaldeans upon them so that they would return to the Lord their God and repossess their promised land. In fact, God forecasts that He "will rejoice over them to do them good, and...will plant them in [the] land assuredly with [His] whole heart and with [His] whole soul."[18] Jeremiah's purchase of the field would demonstrate his trust in the promise of the Lord that one day his descendants would return to the land.

Jeremiah may have floundered within his spirit. What sense did it make to buy land that he couldn't occupy or even control? All Jeremiah could **see** was the surety of advancing armies; but all God **promised** revealed much about the One who would accomplish the task He had initiated, for God quizzed Jeremiah: "Behold, I am the LORD, the God of all flesh: is there any thing too hard for me?"[19] When what we **see** and what God **promises** don't match, **remember that Jesus is Lord.**

Seminars tout it, books market it, speakers promote it, and it sounds something like this: "Bring your people along through relationships until they feel ownership in the church." There is nothing wrong with building relationships with our people or with our community; in fact, such service and commitment produce evident fruit. However, we should commit ourselves to observe the principle of divine ownership as it applies to the local church. Assessments bring to our remembrance that our role is to "take heed...[unto ourselves,] and to all the flock, over the which the Holy Ghost hath made [us] overseers, to feed the church of God, which **he hath purchased with his own blood.**"[20] Sometimes adjustment requires a role change, and we are reminded that we are not the owners of our local church.

It didn't take me long to learn firsthand the public nature of full-time ministry. As a young pastor with a young family, I was tempted to disdain the "fishbowl lifestyle" as a necessary evil. I now, however, appreciate this opportunity, realizing that my fishbowl existence is a privilege—an arena for displaying a heart of love and compassion toward those whom God places in my path and in His church.

Paul sensed the burden and the blessing also when he acknowledged that we are "made a spectacle unto the world, and to angels, and to men."[21]

This word **"spectacle"** being studied is θεατρον, being **interpreted** is "theatre," and being **defined** is "a place for public show,"[22] which we are by God's choosing as we participate with Him in ministry. We are a public show. Our lives are a theatre. It is important to protect our families from certain ministry demands, but do not avoid all scrutiny. Rather, accept it as an opportunity to influence others for Christ. Admittedly, it is difficult to determine a standard that regulates our conduct with regard to issues of transparency and privacy, yet we each must ascertain God's will concerning the matter.

These opportunities to influence others are one avenue of multiplying the ministry. While we will develop this concept in greater detail in Chapter 8, let us consider that multiplication is a Biblical concept. The Spirit of God matures leaders for this reason: that we may reproduce ourselves in others, specifically those whom God is calling and equipping for ministry. This approach may not be immediately applicable to the church-planting pastor who has recently begun his labors, for he is investing his time and effort in the development of new believers. However, as the work matures, leaders can prayerfully recognize lay leaders who can be trained and given authority in the ministry. A minister who allows personal insecurities or mistrust of others or selfishness to dissuade him from this process limits God at the expense of his people.

Every time a leader begets leaders, he doesn't use others to build his authority; he uses his authority to build others. Many ministry stresses are solved by means of leadership training and subsequent delegation of authority. This practice is particularly important with regard to soul winning and discipleship: A leader who develops people **adds.** A leader who develops leaders **multiplies.** The heart of ministry is reaching people with the Gospel and developing them into fully committed followers of Jesus Christ. We shouldn't allow ministry distractions to redirect our energy from our primary purpose. Leadership is not as it appears but as it performs. Godly leadership is still effective during times of stress.

A number of leaders gain nothing more than a reclusive lifestyle from their assessments. They determine that the disappointment and hurt they have experienced in ministry are too much to bear emotionally. They continue in the ministry, but their heart is not open to the Lord or to His people. A loss of faith in people is ultimately a loss of faith in the Lord of the people, who promised that He would perform the good work that He began in them until the day of Christ's reappearing.[23] The ones who shield themselves from the disappointments of ministry by retreating from people break the Law of Love.[24] We are called to a ministry of reconciliation: a ministry of love.[25] Love is:

95

the impelling incentive and motive for all witness
and ministry of love in which [we] are being
trained. For love must share with others or die. It
must give to others all that it received, or it cannot remain love. Love can only live in your heart
as it propagates itself by sharing. Love is the con-
straining power, which makes [His] lovers willing
to go to all lengths, even to death itself, in order
to bring the good news of the love of God to those
who have never heard it, [to water that seed of
love already planted in the hearts of His chosen
ones]. It is love to the Lamb of God who bears the
sins of the world....[26] Love must express itself in
giving; must find a way to become one with others, just as He found a way to give His own life to
us and thereby to become one with us![27]

We cannot become an emotional hermit and still
serve God's people.

Criticism can serve a purpose. Sometimes it's true but
not always. Because of this, our esteem and our confidence are gathered in the security of His love alone. Our
hope is in His promises; our guidance, in His Word; and
our direction, by His Spirit. Covet that relationship and
be strongly rooted there, sheltered by His grace but also
sensitive to His chastisement, which may come at our
expense and be delivered by others.

Two Biblical examples immediately come to mind, and
both happened to the same man—David. Both stories are
quite familiar. The first occurred[28] when his trusted con-
fidant and counselor Nathan, a prophet in the nation of
Israel, confronted an adulterous David. On that sad occasion David would not acknowledge his sin until Nathan
pointed and accused, "Thou art the man"; however, this
confrontation did result in confession and restoration.

The second occurred while David was experiencing
some of the consequences of that first carnal act. Fleeing
from his rebellious son, Absalom, David received the
curses of a passerby named Shimei. Rather than hurl a

few of his own stones back at him (recall that David was a pretty accurate stone-thrower), he responded, "It may be that the LORD will look on [my] affliction, and that the LORD will requite me good for his cursing this day."[29]

On each of these occasions we find a confrontation that could be interpreted as criticism. On the first occasion David was guilty; on the second, innocent. David allowed those who approached him negatively to serve him and considered them instruments in the hand of God for his benefit.

The purpose of assessment is adjustment. Because of this, we may find it necessary to inform our church of the structural or founding principles of our local assembly. People have complained regarding the structure or operations of churches at times without first studying the organizational documents by which they are governed. Their introduction to these principles will reveal that the church is operating in exact accordance with the church constitution. It is good periodically to teach the Biblical basis for the church structure and operational guidelines, so that when adjustments are made, they realize the founding principles are not being forgotten. During one period of assessment we went a step further and wrote a church operational guideline booklet with explanations of various situations for the membership's understanding.

I have witnessed men who, because of extreme adversity in the ministry or perhaps genuine disappointment with authority figures in their lives, have literally changed their doctrinal position. We must never allow our disappointment in people to cause us to deny the principles God entrusted to us during times of real growth and development, if indeed they were derived from Scripture. While there may be legitimate assessments and subsequent changes to be made in method and procedure, it is never right to forsake the founding scriptural position of the church in a time of difficulty. "If the foundations be destroyed, what can the righteous do?"[30]

Growing churches must have clear lines of communication and adequate resources for training new lay and staff leadership as an ongoing part of the ministry. Simply adding or birthing a new Sunday school class or appointing a council for ministering to bereaved members can alleviate stress and serve as a time-management tool for our serving team.

Several years ago I enjoyed a day of sailing on a thirty-six-foot sailboat off the California coast between the Los Angeles Harbor and the Santa Catalina Islands. Clear, cloudless skies; coarse, unforeseen winds—the vessel chopped through the changing waters of the cold Pacific.

A straight track had been charted; however, the gales prevented even the best intentions of the captain. Unable to sail upwind and aware of the frustration of the "dead zone," he mentally calculated the leeway and repeatedly checked and adjusted. Switching the sides of the operating sails expertly, tacking at forty-five-degree angles, he guided us toward the charted destination. His careful response to the influence of the unpredictable winds determined the outcome.

As the winds of the sea force sailing vessels from their plotted course, so Christian leaders encounter strong winds of a rapidly changing culture, a nonstop schedule, inevitable trials and unanticipated disappointments. When the **winds of change** rush upon us, check and adjust, check and adjust. We shouldn't get caught in the "dead zone" only to relinquish our influence in our churches and communities. Charging upwind is impossible, but precision tacking can carry us to our intended destination. By carefully responding to our unpredictable conditions, by relying on the steady and perfect guidance of the Spirit who charts our course, we will be delivered safely to Heaven's shores that we may receive "Well done" from the Captain of our salvation.

Section 3

Establishing Leadership
Requirements

CHAPTER 7

Driver's Seat or Shotgun?
A Discussion of Permits, Licenses and Freedom

Why do fifteen-year-olds start itching for their parents to let them get behind the steering wheel of the family car? They know that within a year or so, they will get a permit and then—glory of all glories—the license: that coveted card, which means—well, what does it mean? Do teenagers want a permit or a license just so they can hold a new form of I.D. in their hands, or is the real motivator freedom?

Freedom invites responsibility. Parents don't usually throw a set of keys at their teenager on the eve of his sixteenth birthday and say, "Have at it. Don't get yourself killed, okay?" On the contrary, parents will take their son or daughter outside, and they will look at the car and discuss its features and probably discuss something about life too and the transition he or she is now making into young adulthood. A spoken or unspoken understanding passes from parent to child that emphatically states: "I'm trusting you. This increased responsibility is a gift of love, and I expect that you will enjoy this freedom and that you will discipline yourself to drive carefully. I love you."

Now let's take a detour. Have you examined the philosophies of grace circulating today? They are not concerned primarily with grace as a means of salvation as much as they are with grace as a means of permission. The new concept of grace promotes a "do-it-yourself" Christianity. It encourages us to read the Bible and accept Jesus, but then we choose how we think we can best enjoy our new relationship. Think up your own rules, establish your own guidelines; or don't choose any at all—just bask in the warm glow of grace. It is an invitation to "come just as you are" and then stay that way.

Current philosophies of grace deemphasize righteous living, and Christians are stumbling under the influence of these unbiblical approaches to the doctrine of grace. Their resulting intoxication with freedom causes them to resent anyone who espouses the belief that **grace should discipline one toward holiness.** "For the grace of God that bringeth salvation hath appeared to all men, Teaching us that, denying ungodliness and worldly lusts, we should live soberly, righteously, and godly, in this present world."[1]

Yes, grace is directional. It is designed to move us in the direction of conformity to the image of God's dear Son, Jesus.

Many have sought to redefine *legalism* or to escape its false label at the expense of solid Biblical principles. Some have adopted a lax attitude toward the spiritual disciplines and family values over which our forefathers in the Faith would have mourned and fasted. They regard the marriage covenant casually, pursue wealth instead of practicing stewardship, make merchandise of the Gospel according to worldly models, neglect the Lord's Day, ignore or speak against Biblical standards and water down the preaching of the Word to avoid possible offense.

Now a permit lasts only a little while, whereas a license is for a lifetime. However, true freedom transcends the temporal and looks toward eternity. An elementary understanding of these basic definitions places the topic of our discussion into sharp focus. Some Christians want only a **permit**. They ask, "Will you permit me to try this while I find out if it is right for me? After all, I'm just working out my own salvation." Unfortunately, they forget the fear and trembling part. "Self-esteem and the fear of God cannot be integrated, and a glance at the church of the nineties leaves no doubt as to which of those has been eliminated."[2]

Those who would desire a permit also appear to neglect the scholarship, devotion and experience of the men and women of our great Christian heritage who learned and then recorded that learning for us in wonderful Christian classics that speak of Christian conduct. A church member might ask his pastor, "Can I have the liberty to see something different than you?" I am a pastor, and I am going to shock you. Yes, a member may have the liberty to see something different than the pastor. However, as a pastor I am going to encourage him to avoid those things that might hinder him in the sanctification process.

Many Christians want to understand freedom as their permit or license to live the way they want to live. They resort to unfriendly and untrue terms, the favorite being *legalistic,* with reference to those who believe that we are disciplined by grace to live a holy life, who would go so far as to say that abstaining from a specific sin would benefit our spiritual growth and discipline. Ministers who provide examples of holiness by preaching about certain types of sin are often misunderstood or misrepresented by people who want their own way.

The permit and license crowd carry their Bibles like identification cards that confirm their Christianity; however, they never experience the freedom Christ intended for His beloved (freedom from the curse of sin). They become a prey to the new grace teaching. It appeals to their tender conscience and becomes a springboard out of the church they attend, a reason to escape the discipline of grace and the sanctification process altogether. They remain spiritual teenagers forever and are trapped in Christian adolescence and apathy.

These "injured ones" often find a home on the couch of a counselor who either promotes the new grace philosophy or denies a real grace experience within the confines of the church. "A false gospel always brings bondage. Our techniques never end; our therapy sessions go on until either our bodies can no longer climb the stairs to the counselor's office or our insurance coverage runs out. Eventually we collapse, bleeding and exhausted,"[3] but not closer to God or nearer the experience of intimacy with Him that His Word promises. "The psychological gospel teaches that I sin because of what others have done to me, that salvation lies in raising my self-worth, and that God is a genie waiting to meet my every need."[4] Leaders should celebrate the liberation of grace understanding, practicing and valuing its relationship to sanctification.

A false idea of freedom is ruining America, and a false idea of grace destroys churches. Freedom isn't free, and it is often the search for liberty (absence of authority) that causes a person to find himself enslaved. Remember the Prodigal Son? He said, "Hey, Dad, I don't want all this mess here. I want my freedom!" He chose his own way, and, yes, he had his freedom. But that freedom ruined his life.

Biblical grace fills up the spiritual gas tank and places believers on the road to spiritual maturity. The new grace leaves an empty tank but promises a full life. People will continue in the habits of their unregenerate past, and they will even have some people assure them that it is okay; however, emptiness is its end. The church that accepts the doctrine of false grace is filled with attendees dependent on support groups rather than servants depending on Jesus.

I challenge you, as grace is being redefined, submit yourself to the discipline of grace and become more like Jesus Christ rather than more like you were before you were saved! In this unstable cultural climate, a servant leader must both model and teach Biblical grace.

The 1950s are gone and with them the pastor's prerogative to stand in his pulpit and order the lifestyle of his parishioners. The church doesn't want orders; they want answers, and each attempt by the pastor to define holiness or promote standards is met with a single question: "Why?" Servant leaders must respond lovingly and with patience, using God's Word both to teach and to illustrate true freedom and grace and how they can be practically applied and enjoyed in one's daily life.

Separation begins in the heart with an attitude toward God prompted by His love and grace. Separation is a Biblical principle that steers Christians away from the potholes of false doctrine and ice patches of licentious practice. The first matter in discussing separation is not "What am I separating from?" but "To whom am I separating?" Biblical separation has both positive and negative aspects—separation is unto Christ as well as away from the world.

Although *separation* has become a word of choice among conservative and independent pastors, I submit that it may be helpful to teach our congregations this Biblical principle by defining and giving examples of how the word *cleave* is used in Scripture. This word is found throughout the Old and New Testaments. A careful word study reveals the word has two distinct meanings.

For example, Jesus said in Mark 10:6, 7, "But from the beginning of the creation God made them male and female. For this cause shall a man leave his father and mother, and **cleave** to his wife." In Deuteronomy 11:22 the Lord commands Israel "to love the LORD your God,...walk in all his ways, and...**cleave** unto him." A modern Webster's dictionary defines *cleave* in this way: "to adhere firmly and closely or loyally and unwaveringly (synonym, to stick)."

In Leviticus 1:17 instructions are given for the offering of a burnt sacrifice. If one brings an offering of turtledoves or of young pigeons, the priest is to "**cleave** it with the wings thereof." Zechariah 14:4 paints a telling picture of the glorious second coming of Christ when "his feet shall stand in that day upon the mount of Olives, which is before Jerusalem on the east, and the mount of Olives shall **cleave** in the midst thereof toward the east and toward the west, and there shall be a very great valley; and half of the mountain shall remove toward the north, and half of it toward the south." The same modern Webster's dictionary quoted from above also offers this second definition of the word *cleave:* "to separate into distinct parts [to make a difference between two groups, views or entities]." It is common for people to recognize and in some cases have a meat cleaver in their own home kitchens.

The purpose for including the result of this word study is to share this: There is a benefit to teaching the Biblical principle of separation by using the word *cleave*. Its dual definition is supported by Scripture, history and modern usage without the connotation of isolationism inherent in the word *separation*. We know that Biblical separation does not avoid contact with the world, only conformity to it. However, those unschooled in the Christian dialect may not be aware of this, and they are the ones that we desire to reach for Christ.

The Bible does not instruct us to deny friendship with the unsaved. How are we going to lead anybody to Christ if we cannot entertain friends who do not know the Lord? Every one of us comes into contact with unsaved people throughout the week. Praise God for that! We are not talking about isolationism. We must be out in the world without conforming to the world.

Just as the man must leave his father and mother and cleave to his wife, so also a growing Christian chooses to leave the habits of his former life and cleave to Christ and the instruction of His Word. We want to **cleave** or stick loyally to our Lord. We want to **cleave** or make a difference between the "world" that God so loved and the "world system" that God so hates. We want to be light and salt in our communities, our faith affecting those around us, not vice versa.

Separation is based upon the principle of avoiding the unequal yoke, the principle that instructs us to respond to the Fatherhood and love of God with a desire to please Him. A Christian whose mind is being renewed each day does not want to get into something that's going to *pull him away from* Christ or Biblical doctrine, that's going to *pull him toward* a sinful pattern. On the contrary, Christians who are growing in the grace and knowledge of the Lord welcome the challenge and invitation to intimacy with Christ through separation. They understand that Biblical separation is *turning away from* sin and *toward* Christ.

The reason God tells us not to get involved in an unequal yoke is that He loves us and covets our fellowship. God expresses His desire: "I want you to be My people. I don't want you to be My people *part* of the time. I want you to be My people *all* the time. I don't want anything pulling you away from Me." If we can effectively communicate this to our church families, they will understand this principle as a tremendous compliment. The reason God forbids the unequal yoke is His love for us, His enjoyment of our fellowship and His commitment to our protection.

In fact, God promises a more intimate relationship to those who are separated unto Him. God assumed the role of Father with joy at the moment of our salvation.

He assures us, promising, "I'm not just going to be your Father in name only—I am going to be your Father in an active, everyday sense." He wants to be an active Father, participating in the growth and development of His dear children and the church family as a whole.

Servant leaders must convey this truth to the church family as God's faithful messengers, especially as it concerns grace. For God's Spirit instructs the adolescent Christian at a crucial moment, saying, "I'm trusting you. The increased responsibility that accompanies grace is a gift of love. I expect that you will enjoy this freedom and that you will discipline yourself to live **grace**-fully. I love you." When Christians read their Bible, the Author is present with them, available to discuss the features of the Christian life, to invite them to spiritual adulthood and maturity. Separation is a brother to grace; however, just as a driver's license by itself accomplishes nothing, likewise separation is meaningless if its purpose is not achieved. The purpose of a license is to drive. The goal of separation is union with Christ—freedom from sin.

We must teach God's children that it is possible for them to draw nigh unto God and that the route is separation. This is a choice. We believe—rather, we experience—God's love and submit to His grace whereby His Spirit is able to create in us a disposition that desires to please Him. We must clearly guide people into the sure knowledge that the Spirit's convictions are deliberate. The purpose of conviction is conformity. Rather than standing by while Christians adopt a fatalistic attitude, whining, "Oh, I can never be close to God," instead, encourage them to deal with it—deal with Him.

Plain old selfishness is the cause of inattentiveness to the ministry of the Spirit. People do not wish to give up the things to which they have assigned a false value, such as an affiliation with an organization, frequent stops at a questionable place of entertainment, relationships with a particular crowd or ill influence and flirtation with a sinful lifestyle. Should we not encourage them to separate from such things and do it boldly, without apology, in love, that they might experience the reality of victorious living in Christ daily?

The job of the pastor is to pray, "Master, Lord, as we establish a church, give us wisdom. Our prayer is that we might establish ourselves as You direct, because You are the Head of this church, and we want this church to please You." God will answer this prayer, and His answer will include change—change in you and change through you to reach the flock He entrusted to you. This will require that you take bold initiatives regarding separation, grace and holiness from a Biblical stance.

Holiness means that there are some things a believer cannot do. People who emphasized their own rights did not build America. America was built by emphasizing responsibility and service. Now that we are asserting our rights, America is falling apart. Have we recognized that churches rise and fall in a similar fashion?

We have a mission to accomplish! We are to win people to Jesus Christ by helping them have a heart for God. If they are in Christ, we believe they ought to be new creatures. Godly pastors and churches through the centuries have tried earnestly, though not perfectly, to warn believers of some things that they cannot do if they will be like Christ. To say that such warnings are a violation of the principle of grace living is unwarranted by Scripture. The problem is that some Christians use *liberty* as their code word or rationale for a rebellious heart—a password used to justify a rebellious lifestyle. Herein lies the danger of abusing and redefining Christian liberty. Liberty is simply freedom from sin and freedom to serve Christ from a genuine heart of love. It is not an excuse to live a lifestyle that quenches the Holy Spirit.

We often hear the terms *principle, conviction* and *standard*. What do they mean? A **principle** is a Bible truth I must live by. A **conviction** is a personal belief based upon a Bible principle. A **standard** is a policy that helps me keep my conviction. When we learn Bible principles, we gain Bible convictions and then establish Bible-based standards so we can live a life that pleases the Lord Jesus Christ. This is basic Christianity.

The standard is not the goal; pleasing Jesus is the goal. We need to realize that we cannot shirk from it. We cannot preach any less. That's not God's calling. May God help us to be sensitive to His Word and His Spirit as we develop godly standards by which our testimony is manifest before a lost world. Model grace before your church family as one who gives his will, his emotions and his full attention to the impulses of God's Spirit.

Some people, in an effort to speed past the set limits of **true grace and freedom**, commit moving violations; and while the comparison is stated, why do you think police officers issue moving violations? Is it not because the reckless speed of offenders is a danger to the safety of other drivers? In a similar manner, Christians who commit moving violations endanger their environment: the spiritual climate in their churches and the potential for effective witness by these churches in their communities. Real-life speeding tickets require a price to be paid. Speeding Christians incur a price that their churches and the Christian community as a whole will pay in loss of respect or, worse, a charge of hypocrisy.

Some people speed, and others take off past licentiousness into rebellious sin. They may not say it verbally, but their actions speak loudly enough. They conduct themselves in such a way as if to flaunt "I can tempt my Christian brother and sister because I have liberty. I can liberate them too." I have dealt with several cases when one Christian has said to another, "We can do this questionable thing or that sin and still be okay in the Christian life, because we have liberty." The Apostle Peter dubbed them "false teachers" and apparently had run into a few of them; for he said, "They speak great swelling words of vanity," such as "I have been saved for a long time. I have known God for a long time, so let me help you to further enjoy the Word of God so that you are not held down."

Let me be clear—one's lifestyle will never change that person's standing with God. If you are truly saved, then positionally you are sanctified and sealed before a mighty God, and nothing can change that. However, there is such a thing as daily sanctification. It does matter to God how you live, and it is imperative that leaders live their lives in awe and respect of God. Bible liberty gives us freedom to obey the Lord and honor His name.

Do we exist to win people to the Lord? I have committed my entire life to this cause. My heart breaks to see anyone in the church pulling Christians one inch back from where Christ has brought them. We must be careful that our churches, our activities and our homes do not become stumbling blocks to those who may be struggling with particular problems. We should use our liberty to instruct God's people and to exhort them to get people *to* church, not *away from* it.

Paul says, 'Take heed lest by any means you abuse your liberty and become a stumbling block' (I Cor. 8:9). There are weaker brothers who are observing us as their example. We need to be careful that we do not inadvertently harm their spiritual growth. With compassion, yet swiftly and privately, we need to counsel those within our churches who violate the law of liberty, encouraging them to slow down and enjoy the blessing of grace without becoming a roadblock to someone else's growth.

The Bible is a mirror, and when we look into this mirror, God often reveals changes for our good. Few people look in a mirror, even in passing, without making a small adjustment—straightening a tie, pushing a wisp of hair back in place. James exhorted, "Be ye doers of the word, and not hearers only, deceiving your own selves. For if any be a hearer of the word, and not a doer, he is like unto a man beholding his natural face in a glass: For he beholdeth himself, and goeth his way, and straightway forgetteth what manner of man he was."[5]

Do you know what the law of liberty is? It is the Bible, specifically the New Testament. Therefore, understanding and enjoying liberty come only when a Christian obeys the Bible—the perfect example of liberty. Old-fashioned preaching and Bible-based convictions are a church family's best friends. These foundations keep our congregations from rotting in the jail of stunted spiritual growth.

We cannot study grace without coming to Romans, chapter 6—a discourse on the holy life of a believer. Romans, chapter 6, is not primarily about grace but about what grace produces in a person's life.

Guard against any teaching of grace which deemphasizes holy living; "for there are certain men crept in unawares, who...[turn] the grace of our God into lasciviousness."[6]

There are two schools of thought about grace. One school of Biblical thought maintains that as one understands God's grace, it will discipline that one to live a life that is more Christlike. Discipline requires self-control; however, *self-control* can be a misleading term. Self-controlled by what? I suggest that Biblical self-control is control by love, His love, which constrains us and shelters us in its completeness. The Bible says it is possible to live a life that grieves the Holy Spirit. But by God's grace it is also possible to live a life that pleases Him.

Some may say, "Hey, I have liberty to do what I want to do and to go where I want to go!" The Apostle Paul cast his vote—such people are abusers of the liberty that we have in Christ. A genuine understanding of Christian liberty invites us to ask, "Lord, how can I serve You? How can I be enslaved to You? Lord, how can I serve someone else?" That is the mature Christian response to Christian liberty.

"For if we have been planted together in the likeness of his death, we shall be also in the likeness of his resurrection."[7]

"I am crucified with Christ: nevertheless I live; yet not I, but Christ liveth in me: and the life which I now live in the flesh I live by the faith of the Son of God, who loved me, and gave himself for me."[8]

We are crucified with Christ. **When Jesus died, we died.** His flesh was crucified on a cross. Under grace I understand that my will is nailed to that same cross. This understanding is the key to my living victoriously in Him.

Many Christians, under the guise of grace, are digging up the old life. They are digging up what Jesus buried. I can exercise my freedom and call it liberty, but dissatisfaction results when I am not identifying with His death, burial and resurrection. **Our identity is in Him.**

"And hath raised us up together, and made us sit together in heavenly places in Christ Jesus."[9]

Have you noticed many children hate spinach when they are growing up but when they are grown they enjoy eating it raw in a salad? Their appetite changes, and so does the appetite of a growing Christian. The saved man doesn't grumble, "How can I find a religious reason to go backwards?" A saved man rejoices, "I can grow in God's grace and become more like my Lord. I have new appetites and desires now. I am seated up here in the heavenlies with Jesus Christ. I want to experience the resurrected life. Get these graveclothes off of me!"

"How shall we, that are dead to sin, live any longer therein?"

"Likewise reckon ye also yourselves to be dead indeed unto sin, but alive unto God through Jesus Christ our Lord."[10]

Under grace I **reckon** myself dead unto sin. *Reckon* means to estimate or compute that I already have the victory in Jesus Christ. It means get up daily and affirm, "I am crucified with Christ. I am reckoning myself dead indeed unto sin. I am recognizing what happened at Calvary. Lord Jesus, as I reckon myself dead unto sin, I ask You to let me be alive to Your will for my life today. Help me, God, be alive to You because of Your graciousness in saving me. I don't want to live for myself anymore. I want to live for You today, Lord."

If we are self-centered, we are missing the purpose of grace—a God-centered life. Reckoning oneself as dead to sin involves establishing what is right and wrong. If I am going to reckon myself dead indeed unto sin, I had better know what sin is. Herein lies the great controversy. Herein is the great difference among many pastors and churches today. Should a pastor, a school or a college set a guideline for something that may be sinful? New grace teachers say, "Oh, no! That would be a list." A "Christian" form of relativism prevails with new grace teachings; for while one is encouraged to reckon oneself dead unto sin, he also must decide what is sin for him and what is not.

I believe it does not matter whether it is suggested from a pulpit or a parent: God directs us primarily by His Word but also through God-given realms of authority. Pastors should encourage their people to pay credence to these authorities, specifically the authority of the Word of God for **faith** and **practice**. I think that pastors should raise a standard. We need to say, "Folks, if we are going to reckon ourselves dead indeed unto sin, we need to know what sin is!" Leadership needs to set Biblical guidelines to help people reach spiritual maturity.

Do restrictions rob us of joy? We are told that man-made rules and restrictions, passed off as Biblical, become joy-killers. Those who defend the standards of living which they believe are based on scriptural principles are accused of being guilty of petty concerns and critical suspicions. They are also called stern, rigid and coldhearted—the proponents of a legalistic style of strong-arm teaching.

What about the doctrine espoused in Romans, chapter 6? Is the topic of this discourse emancipation from rules? No! It is about living a holy and godly life for Jesus Christ, a part of which is going to involve living by convictions based on Biblical principles.

Five times in this chapter Christians are commanded to yield or surrender themselves to Christ. **Our response should be** "Lord, I want to surrender my life to You completely. You have saved me by Your grace, Lord. Help me to surrender my will to You." We should not say, "You have saved me by Your grace; now because of Your grace, let me have my own way." Instead, we should pray, "Help me surrender; help me yield." **Being saved by grace does not give us an excuse to sin; it gives us a reason to obey.**

The New Testament is not about what we can or cannot do but what Christ can do in and through us by His grace. We certainly do not intend to major on the minors in our ministry. Our goal is to lift up Christ. However, we must not minimize the fact that Christ is worthy of our best—He wants our lives to be totally consecrated to Him.

"Stand fast therefore in the liberty wherewith Christ hath made us free, and be not entangled again with the yoke of bondage. Behold, I Paul say unto you, that if ye be circumcised, Christ shall profit you nothing. For I testify again to every man that is circumcised, that he is a debtor to do the whole law. Christ is become of no effect unto you, whosoever of you are justified by the law; ye are fallen from grace. For we through the Spirit wait for the hope

of righteousness by faith. For in Jesus Christ neither circumcision availeth any thing, nor uncircumcision; but faith which worketh by love. Ye did run well; who did hinder you that ye should not obey the truth?"[11]

The word *liberty* means "freedom from bondage." Paul's reference to 'falling from grace' does not mean Christians were losing their salvation. **It means they were simply making salvation of no effect in their daily lives.** However, our salvation should affect us—every aspect of our lives. God's grace should affect our preaching and teaching—our entire approach to ministry and God's people. God has purchased His church as His own special possession, a peculiar people of His own choosing. Like a Father—our Father—He wants to discipline us as we continue in our spiritual journey.

As a pastor I know that internal and external forces exist which can frighten us from pursuing the love of Christ and allowing His love to enliven our witness and service. One such external pressure is the ecumenical craze. Our flesh wants to be part of a large ecumenical movement because of the acceptance we find in it. Flesh cringes at the prospect of reproach. Ego desires popularity with everyone all the time. It's okay to admit that we enjoy the accolades and acceptance of our peers. There is nothing wrong with acceptance as long as we do not allow it to become a source of vanity, of temptation toward compromising our Biblical beliefs.

The point is that if we are going to be Christlike leaders, then we need to take a stand and bear some reproach. Reproach may occur because of our personal convictions or the convictions of our church regarding the apostasy and false religion of the day. Our purpose is to feed His sheep. The pastors who are moving in the fast lane of compromise are putting themselves in the driver's seat—arbitrarily determining what is important and what is not for their own purposes rather than the purposes that Christ has expressed in His Word.

Personally, I prefer riding "shotgun." After all, He is the Great Shepherd; I am the undershepherd. He is the Driver; I am a passenger in this journey of grace. I must fully submit in grace to the leadership of my Lord, even when He leads me along a narrow path. He is the Way, leading me in the paths of righteousness, disciplined by grace, growing in grace and teaching grace to others for His name's sake.

CHAPTER 8

Spirit-filled Semantics

Take time to be holy—the world rushes on.
Spend much time in secret with Jesus alone.
By looking to Jesus, like Him thou shalt be;
Thy friends in thy conduct His likeness shall see.[1]

The world rushes on and we are rushing with it. The influences shaping our world on a larger scale are reproducing themselves on a smaller but no less significant scale. Thus, what occurs in the world is being felt in our churches. So if we must choose one word that defines what has been and is occurring in our world, then I think the word is *redefinition.* In the world this creates havoc and results in relativism as people define for themselves what is right, wrong and, more importantly, convenient. In our churches this causes confusion among believers about our purpose and results in a "Christian relativism" as believers define for themselves what is Biblical, unbiblical and, unfortunately, convenient.

The precious hymn quoted at the beginning of this chapter reminds Christians of their purpose—that is, to be holy, separated unto Christ, in a rushing world that is passing away. This hymn further instructs that only "by looking to Jesus" and spending time with Him in prayer and in the Word are we transformed into His likeness—a likeness acknowledged or at least noticed by others. This seems to beg the question, "What is Christ's likeness?" How should leaders practically teach believers the characteristics of Christlikeness?

A traditional tool of instruction has been the incorporation of core values and leadership requirements based upon Biblical principles. However, in our current world and church climate prone to redefinition, we discover that much confusion exists among the ranks of believers concerning where doctrine begins and ends, also how the principles derived from doctrine should positively affect the lifestyle of those belonging to Christ. It is time for a return to Spirit-filled semantics: In this chapter we will seek the **Biblical meanings and relationships** that exist between the doctrine, core values and leadership requirements of a local church.

Doctrine is the systematic presentation of Biblical truth, which does not change from one country to another because it originates with God in His Word and is applied by God's people—His ambassadors or representatives on earth. Doctrine is the same yesterday, today and forever, based on Christ who is unchanging. This is its greatest strength. The fact that people everywhere do not always look to Jesus as their doctrinal Authority is the greatest enemy to doctrinal purity.

The church is "in the world" (found on all continents). And it is doctrinal truth, the truths of the Gospel, which binds believers together across all physical boundaries and is the substance that keeps them from being "of the world" (John 17:11, 14). Therefore, it is the responsibility of spiritual leaders to communicate doctrine to people.

In the case of an existing church, it is not a matter of establishing the doctrine so much as connecting people to the foundational doctrines of the Bible. In this hour when many believe doctrine is unimportant and "too divisive," it is time for spiritual leaders to act, recognizing that what one believes determines how one behaves.

True doctrine does indeed divide: it divides light from darkness, right from wrong, and life from death. It also unites. God's love cannot be known or appropriated by sinful men without the involvement of doctrine.[2]

Leaders who are not committed to the truth of the Word will not develop ministries that stand the test of eternity.

A commitment to doctrine, to the "faith...once delivered unto the saints,"[3] is the vital dynamic in a growing church. Commitment to Christ is the center of all God-honoring ministries; for Christ is the "express image,"[4] the exact representation, of the Father, and through Him we are reconciled to the Father and invited to know Him in a way we cannot experience apart from the Son. Therefore, His Word is the basis for the teaching (the doctrine) that holds the church together. Experiences and emotions won't last; management styles and outreach programs change; but God's Word is Truth and always relevant to people, because doctrine is not for the benefit of God but for the benefit of God's people, that they might know Him, which is eternal life.[5]

The counsel of Scripture faithfully guides and warns men to take heed to **the doctrine.** Consider Paul's teaching concerning various duties of the believers in I Thessalonians 5:16–23:

"Rejoice evermore. Pray without ceasing. In every thing give thanks: for this is the will of God in Christ Jesus concerning you. Quench not the Spirit. Despise not prophesyings. Prove all things; hold fast that which is good. Abstain from all appearance of evil. And the very God of peace sanctify you wholly; and I pray God your whole spirit and soul and body be preserved blameless unto the coming of our Lord Jesus Christ."

The context of this passage reveals that Paul, instructing the believers concerning prophetic utterances, warns them to test all public declarations of doctrine (prove all things). Whenever some new teaching is manifest (makes an appearance), the content of that prophetic message is to be compared with what is known about the character and work of God—the doctrine or teaching concerning Him. What is consistent with that teaching is to be accepted (held fast), and that which is contrary to His teaching is to be rejected (abstained from).

Paul taught this consistently. In Romans 12:9 he cautioned, "Abhor that which is evil; cleave to that which is good." It is a valid inference to state that Paul made a distinction between true doctrine and false. The church has its foundation in Christ; therefore, no vacancy for doctrinal individualism exists.

We must resolutely guard against modern proneness to casual individualism. Exploding denominationalism is [only] one example. According to the *World Christian Encyclopedia* (1982) there were an estimated 1,900 Christian denominations at the beginning of the twentieth century and an estimated 22,000 at the end.[6] This projected increase in doctrinal individualism reveals an awful statistic: five new denominations are born each week. What is the moral to this story? Confusion ends when the Bible is not only viewed but also embraced as our authority for faith and practice.

True doctrine and its source is to know Him and His Word. A great deal of Paul's ministry centered upon unfolding that mystery, which is Christ, in whom dwells "all the fulness of the Godhead bodily."[7] It follows that today's servant leader must focus on knowing Christ and His Word. Then he must communicate and connect his people to the reality and revelation of these doctrines, which have proven dynamic in their capacity to transform cultures and individual lives both presently and in history.

In addition to doctrinal commitment, there must also be some **core values** which are generally accepted in ministry. They are the outgrowth of the doctrinal commitment and are based upon Biblical values and patterns. For example, as we considered the passage from I Thessalonians 5:16–23, we noted the clear instruction concerning the acceptance of good Biblical teaching and the rejection of evil teaching that is contrary to the Word of God. However, as we apply those verses to our everyday lives, we may find it helpful to "abstain from all appearance of evil" both in doctrine **and in deed.** This application allows that "evil" includes both false teaching and false living, which result in a lifestyle marked by sinful habits that hinder the testimony of Christ in the local church and its community.

In 1986 as we prepared for our first service in Lancaster, California, my wife, Terrie, and I sat down at the computer to create our first bulletin. We stated that the Lancaster Baptist Church was committed to the Word of God (we did not accept charismatic doctrine), evangelism, missions and a godly testimony. **These values were mentioned often, and they ultimately became our known distinctives throughout our city.**

They have functioned and continue to serve in two capacities: One, they promote community within our local church because as a body of believers we share not only a common faith but also a common application of that faith in our daily lives. Second, they increase the effectiveness of our testimony in our community. Our neighbors know what we believe and how that belief affects our lives. The process and patience necessary for communicating doctrine and core values continue to this day through our teaching and preaching ministries.

Related to core values and Biblical doctrines, yet distinct from them, are **leadership requirements** which are a family or staff matter. I say "staff" because they concern our church leadership team at both the paid and volunteer levels. Certainly these qualifying factors concerning the practice of the church staff may share characteristics with the leadership requirements of other local churches, but this is immaterial. Every local team must have clearly defined leadership requirements.

The Bible clearly commands that a pastor be above reproach, the husband of one wife, self-controlled, a model of good behavior, hospitable, apt to teach, not addicted to wine or greedy, but gentle, considerate, free from the love of money. He must manage his own home well including his relationships with his children. He should not be a new convert, and he must have a good reputation with those outside of the church family. Deacons also should be serious-minded, not gossips or backbiters, not addicted to wine or greedy, but be generally above reproach.[8] However, what about those people who fulfill the extremely important roles, both paid and volunteer, who are not pastors or deacons?

There may be those in your church or organization who argue that any requirement outside of the Biblical requirements mentioned above is restrictive or even sinful. Always, as mentioned in Chapter 6, there is a lobbyer publicly crying out that "if the Bible does not address an issue specifically, then we are not required to discuss or apply any dogmatic teaching in that area." Unfortunately, there are several issues which are not even mentioned in Scripture; however, we can approach them according to Biblical principles in a similar way as we would core values.

In reality every church across denominational lines has leadership requirements, whether or not they admit it. Whether you refer to it as leadership requirements or a covenant, every successful organization has this concept in place, and it is normally in writing.

NBA coach Pat Riley, in his book *The Winner Within,* speaks about the importance of a team covenant: "Every team must decide, very consciously, to uphold covenant terms that represent the best of values....The greatness flowing through the heart of the team must be pumped out to all the extremities."[9]

For example, will you allow a male youth choir worker to wear an earring or a nose ring? It is the responsibility of the pastor to help form the lives of God's people spiritually. It is the responsibility of leaders to aid the process of developing fully committed disciples in the local church, and the attitude and actions they display make a difference.

It is at this point in the development of this topic that dissenters will label our practices as "modeling," their tone indicating a strong disapproval of modeling as a method. They feel that modeling lends the pastor too much power; that he becomes essentially the conscience for his flock; that his list actually functions as a prerequisite for acceptance and love by him, the church family and consequently by Christ (as if that were even possible). They accuse him of modeling legalism. They point their finger and denounce his message, asserting that his list binds people to a yoke of slavery that causes them to become stunted in their Christian growth. Such believers are victimized as they learn to take cues from people who want to produce clones of themselves rather than encouraging believers to be conformed to the image of Christ. The dissenters condemn modeling and lists and emphatically state that the absence of both frees the Lord to direct the spiritual lives of the church family.

Let it be clearly stated, **lists are for leaders.** Their context is the staff. Remember that doctrine is universal. Core values are for the community of believers in the local church and the community your church occupies as a means of testimony; and following this are leadership requirements, a family or staff matter. We cannot expect an unsaved visitor to act like a saved member. We cannot expect a baby believer to act like a mature one. Just as we allow God to invite them into a closer personal walk with

Him marked by spiritual maturity, we also allow Him to invite them into leadership roles. *We do not **choose** them; we **recognize** them.*

In the church at Antioch, Barnabas and Paul ministered faithfully for many years. The Bible records that "as they [the prophets and teachers of the church at Antioch] ministered to the Lord, and fasted, the Holy Ghost said, Separate me Barnabas and Saul for the work whereunto I have called them." [10] The leadership at Antioch obeyed God's leading and sent Barnabas and Paul out. Likewise, when we choose leaders we are not really choosing; we are merely recognizing what God has been and is doing in those individuals' lives and participating in their preparation and execution of the ministry to which God has called them. Once they accept a position of influence, they willingly submit to the limitations required for that office. It may be a matter of conviction or of integrity. We know that Paul and Barnabus limited themselves that they might be effective ministers of Christ. Why do people scream, "Legalist!" when we adopt these principles with a clear conscience, applying them in our own cultural moment as well as we are able?

We have already mentioned Paul, but let him speak for himself: "For our gospel came not unto you in word only, but also in power, and in the Holy Ghost, and in much assurance; **as ye know what manner of men we were among you for your sake. And ye became followers of us, and of the Lord.**" [11] Hmmm...sounds like modeling to me. Our practice of modeling is not a power play; it's discipleship. We recognize that the maturity of every believer is God's work. He is the Vine; we are the branches. We consider it imperative, therefore, that leaders live lives that young believers can follow. As the leader follows after Christ, so the young believer discerns a pattern and is encouraged to imitate Christ, not the leader, knowing that what Christ calls us to, He also enables us to do.

So this begs the question: what does God call us to? He calls us unquestionably to holiness. Peter made this clear, instructing,

"Gird up the loins of your mind, be sober, and hope to the end for the grace that is to be brought unto you at the revelation of Jesus Christ; As obedient children, not fashioning yourselves according to the former lusts in your ignorance: But as he which hath called you is holy, so be ye holy in all manner of conversation; Because it is written, Be ye holy; for I am holy." [12]

Respected theologian G. Campbell Morgan eloquently stated that "the human is to make its progress from innocence to holiness." [13] **Standards are not holiness, but in the context of the church family, they create an environment conducive to holiness. Standards are not the goal; Jesus is the goal.**

The best Biblical argument for leadership requirements is in Corinthians when Paul confessed that all things were lawful for him, but not all things were expedient or profitable in the carrying out of his ministry. It should be noted that the focus of ministry should be on the people being ministered to and not on the inconveniences of the minister or staff member. Any other motivation, regardless of how it is packaged, is a self-centered approach to ministry.

In the area of establishing requirements for leaders in the local church, some practical guidelines may be helpful:

1) If an area is not mentioned specifically in Scripture, then make sure you are operating with a Biblical principle as you teach the leadership requirements of the church. The following Scriptures are helpful: Romans 12:1,2; I Thessalonians 5:22; I Corinthians 10:31. Don't lower the standards. Develop a philosophy of communicating them more effectively, patiently. People want to know why they should act in a certain way.

2) Emphasize the importance of a right heart relationship with God as the central theme of the ministry. An external focus alone creates a shallow membership and a self-righteous attitude. It is true, however, that someone with a tender heart for God will reflect that heart in his outward testimony.

3) Don't rush people into leadership. Most people will come to a place where they will desire meaningful involvement. Allow God to bring them to that place.

4) Don't expect everyone to agree with leadership requirements. People in society resist such guidelines, and sometimes people in the church will respond similarly.

5) Develop a godly atmosphere in the church by modeling holy living rather than merely demanding it.

6) Meet with prospective leaders personally and discuss the level of commitment predetermined by your existing church leadership. Encourage and foster an environment for questions, and allow them time to pray.

7) Balance your leadership requirements with admonitions toward godliness as well as challenges to avoid the evil of this world. Romans 1:1 tells us that the Apostle Paul was separated unto the Gospel of Christ.

8) Allow lay leaders to resign freely from a position at any time without pressuring them to stay. Do not place a "guilt trip" on them if for some reason they need a break. There is nothing wrong with making sure they are not upset or with encouraging them to get involved again when possible; but give them room, even if you feel they are making a mistake.

9) Make sure that you and your team of leaders are liv-

ing by the standard you raise. People would rather see a sermon than hear a sermon any day. John Locke has said, "I have always thought the actions of men the best interpreters of their thoughts."

10) Establish a clear course of discipleship in the church and require all potential leaders to fulfill the discipleship course prior to becoming involved in ministry. It is helpful to teach potential leaders how to identify their spiritual gifts for ministry prayerfully during the discipleship course.

11) Stay true to your convictions. While methodologies may vary and personal preferences are not paramount, we must be true to godly commitments. Any church or organization that turns from its God-given foundation is announcing spiritual doom. They may grow numerically after the change, but compromising scriptural convictions will ultimately bring harm to the testimony of Christ.

A few years ago, a family that was reached and discipled through our church ministry began to withdraw and "chill" spiritually. Their joy in serving the Lord diminished, and their spirit changed over time. Finally they stopped coming to church altogether, and our attempts to visit and bring them back to the flock were misconstrued and unappreciated. As a pastor I was disappointed but felt I had done my best and committed their situation to the Lord in prayer.

A few years later, the same family returned to our church. At first they visited infrequently, and then they came to see me. They shared with me their spiritual struggle, both before they left our church and after they were gone. They indicated a desire to return to our fellowship, and, of course, we gladly welcomed them back. This family shared that when they were out of fellowship with the Lord, even while attending our church, they began to resent the stand of the church on certain issues, and they did not agree with the faithfulness requirements for leaders.

Sitting in my office, now restored to our church and, more importantly, to a tenderhearted relationship with God, the man said to me, "By the way, whatever you do, please don't change your stand, your convictions or your preaching. Our family needs the challenge and appreciates the consistency." In the long run, a community will respect your consistency even if they don't support your position.

Is the church of Christ ready to meet the challenges of the third millennium of Christianity? Are servant leaders sufficiently gripped by the Gospel to address issues ranging from modesty to homosexuality in a Biblical and compassionate manner? The modern Christian and the churches are capitulating on hundreds of issues. Rise up, spiritual leader. Call the church back to Biblical doctrine in order that it may be salt in the world. Establish core values that your church may light its community with a genuine Christian witness expressive of the Spirit of Christ, which invites people to come just as they are to the Lamb of God. Commit to scriptural leadership requirements that your church family may have a lighted path to journey, a fellowship focused upon Christ and committed to His call to follow Him.

Section 4

A Vision for Spiritual
Leadership

CHAPTER 9

Twilight Zone

Down in the human heart, crushed by the tempter,
Feelings lie buried that grace can restore;
Touched by a loving heart, wakened by kindness,
Chords that are broken will vibrate once more.[1]

"Submitted for your approval. You are traveling through another dimension, not of sight and sound but of mind. A journey whose boundaries are that of imagination—your next stop...the Twilight Zone." This phrase from wordsmith Rod Serling, whose dramatic flare captured a generation of TV viewers, is instantly familiar to us. In fact, when we hear it, we all start singing the catchy theme song that accompanied the climactic opener.

I like this classic introduction, but I would prefer to change a few words: "Submitted for your approval. You are traveling through a present dimension of sight and sound but not of belief. A journey whose boundaries are faith plus all power—your present habitation...the Twilight Zone." Do you know the definition of *twilight?* I looked it up in my Webster's dictionary and found two primary meanings, one I didn't expect:

> Twi-light (twī'līt') n. 1. The soft, diffused light cast by the sun when it is below the horizon, esp. following sunset. 2. A PERIOD OR STATE OF DECLINE.

I find both of these definitions intriguing and applicable to the present spiritual climate of America. We are living in a period of spiritual decline. I know that the daytime talk shows and national polls would disagree. The statistics claim that America is becoming more and more "spiritual" daily. However, spirituality differs vastly from spiritual truth; and yet the Son, full of compassion, is casting His vision through His "diffusers of light" as we anticipate His return, not building ministries in our comfort zone but responding to the near-darkness of the twilight with courage and ever-increasing faith in our race towards our forever Home.

Yes, we are in a spiritual race. You might have felt you were the only one who struggled to keep pace with the unending demands on his own emotions, mental strength and time placed upon him by his church or his ministry. But it's not just you; it's all of us. It's the Christian life, and this is how it is supposed to be because we are in a race.

But to where are we racing? And in what manner are we leading the people God has entrusted to us in this race? Without a vision, people perish. They don't complete the race. Some don't even start.

It was a preacher who first espoused this truth for God. His name was Solomon, and he warned, "Where there is no vision, the people perish: but he that keepeth the law, happy is he."[2] Was Solomon referring to a goal or ambition when he spoke of vision? Context accompanied by study determines the matter. The word "vision" being interpreted is "divine instruction." The word "law" in the same verse means "God's words to His people."

As is common in many proverbs, we see a parallelism established, this one being antithetical or contrasting. The words "vision" and "law" are used interchangeably, both referring specifically to God's Word or scriptural insight and understanding. The first line of the verse reveals the fate of those **without scriptural insight:** they perish. The second line of the verse confirms the experience of those **with scriptural insight:** they are happy.

Vision is a corporate buzzword. Companies seek to define where they are and where they are going so that they can post it on the wall and circulate it by office memoranda. They itemize their desires and chart paths to achieve their goals. And the key idea for secular visionaries is accomplishment: What can we accomplish this fiscal year or this quarter? **Vision is "in."**

Now stop and read this carefully: when I speak of vision I am not referring to that which I want to accomplish or goals I set. Rather, I commit myself to hearing, believing and obeying **God's truth** and communicating **that vision** to others.

I remember an article I read about a company of architects and executives of the Disney Corporation, who gathered at Disney World in Orlando, Florida on the eve of its grand opening. They were seated in an area of extraordinary view that overlooked the entire grounds—beautiful. During the ceremonies, one speaker regretted the fact that Walt Disney himself could not be present with them for he had already passed away. Another man kindly corrected him, "Oh, you don't understand. He's already seen all of this. He saw it in his mind before we ever began building."

This illustrates a common application of vision: seeing something that does not yet exist or understanding visually something to come. Conversely, **spiritual vision equals Biblical truth.** And where there is no vision, people perish. The Biblical word "perish" being interpreted is "to cast off restraint." To paraphrase, **where there is no scriptural understanding or insight, the people cast off restraint; they run wild.**

Why was the Prophet Samuel called a seer? A seer was one who could see, one who possessed scriptural understanding. A seer delivered to the people a message from God. He cast vision that caused people to avoid perishing. In fact, during Samuel's infancy the Scriptures testify that "the word of the LORD was precious in those days; there was no **open vision.**"[3] The Word of God was unavailable to the people, little known and rarely obeyed. But "Samuel grew, and the LORD was with him, and did let none of his words fall to the ground."[4] And Samuel shared those words he had caught from God and cast them to the people, helping them to see things that without God's Word they would have been unable to see. Likewise, a man or woman of God is to be one of vision—one who understands what the will and the Word of God are.

Why are our cities languishing? Why are our inner cities hopeless, drug-infested and crime-ridden? It is because there is not enough Bible being preached. It is because there are not enough adult Bible classes and children's Bible classes available to minister to them. **It is because not enough vision is being cast.** The people in our cities are perishing. There are enough alcohol and drugs, but there is not enough Bible. There is enough fornication but not enough faith on the part of God's people to cast more vision. This is why we need to love them and win them and disciple them and include them. This is why we need to send more missionaries. Where there is no Bible entering a community or a nation, people are perishing. Who is going to carry his Bible in there?

Vision is not the pastor's idea. Vision is the Word of God. Now if a pastor is encouraged and guided by the Word of God from which ideas are developed, then the foundation is God's Word, and true vision is the result. And the pastor must assess this vision in the mirror of God's Word, **for there is no understanding of self apart from the Bible.** How we envision ourselves is insignificant. What is paramount is that we envision *through the Bible.* Spiritual vision is a look at one's life through the lens of God's Word.

The true spiritual visionary is one whose eyes have been enlightened by the Word of God, whose heart and mind are soaked with His counsel so filling him that it overflows from his mouth. Where there is a vision in congruence with scriptural insight, then and only then are we rescuing the perishing and caring for the dying as we participate with Him who is merciful, glorifying Jesus who saves.

This is a holy vision, a godly ambition, not a fleshly one. The flesh always heads for the "in" zone, but godly vision is the Word of God alive in our hearts as we sprint towards the end zone dodging potential tackles in pursuit of the goal line. We should prayerfully ask, "Where do You want me to finish this year? What would You have me do? Where should I lead our church family in the Word of God? Help us with the development of the lives of Your people. Help us with the development of the ministry of the local church." **The answer to all of these petitions is vision.**

A clear vision begins with Christ as He reveals His will by His Spirit through His Word, prayer, circumstances and the body of believers. It teaches us to **inspire** God's people to develop a heart for God. It prompts us to **include** new believers in the family of God. It admonishes us to **instruct** them in the precepts of the Faith. It challenges us to **involve** them in ministry. The result is a church whose **impact** touches a community and the world for Christ. These are courageous actions that effect a change in people's lives. Our ministry may not be big, our congregations not large, but our part is critical because it affects people for whom Christ died.

Vision has distinguishing characteristics, the first of which is compassion. I think sometimes that we forget that others are lost, or we choose not to think about it because the reality overwhelms us. There are so many people, emotionally, physically and mentally hurting. Only God can heal them, but without God's people ready to cast that healing vision, they will not discover the acceptance of Christ who loves them just as they are. In fact, their despair is the pathway to their deliverance.

There is also another kind of hurting, probably better understood by the word *unknowing*. A current generation named by a Pepsi commercial "Generation Next" is being reared without a moral or spiritual knowledge of God. Rather than accusing them for their spiritual waywardness, staring rudely at the profusion of their body art, piercing, dress code and music culture—go get them. After all, it was their parents and grandparents whose vote or lack thereof allowed things like the Bible and prayer to be removed from their schools without so much as a showing or dispute. The Gospel changes lives. Don't dismiss a life as wasted or devoid of understanding unless you've personally cast vision for that person, giving him an opportunity to understand the possibility of another life different from the one which he now lives.

The head coach of the Duke University men's basketball team, Mike Krzyzewski, addressing retired alumni, acknowledged that things are in a big mess in the American family today. Things are in too big of a mess for people to be sitting around playing bridge or moving to some retirement community in Florida. He spoke about the need for the wisdom, patience and free time of people who would adopt the young men in his program and responsibly love and help them. He said that the greatest need in his players' lives was for a father, not a coach. They needed someone to teach them how to live.

This man continued to relate the difficulty in just keeping his players sober and clear of date rape charges—the commitment required to help them live semi-clean lives so they could get onto the court and play basketball. But their real need is not another three-point shot; it is a personal faith in Jesus Christ. That is the victory—the only victory able to overcome the world and all of its temptations.

Whether we attempt to cast vision for the college basketball star or the child who attends our neighborhood Bible club, we must have courage. We must realize the insufficiency of borrowed beliefs and develop our own convictions. We must find our sufficiency in His grace and the promise of His power and authority which preceded His command for us to go and visit our neighbors, canvass the university campus, enter the inner cities and preach the Gospel to each one of His creation. Proceed as Moses did, "**seeing him** who is invisible" (Heb. 11:27). We must take our marching orders from the Captain of the Host, as Joshua did, emboldened by these words:

"*Every place that the sole of your foot shall tread upon, that have I given unto you.*"

"*Only be thou strong and very courageous, that thou mayest observe to do according to all the law...turn not from it to the right hand or to the left, that thou mayest prosper whithersoever thou goest. This book of the law shall not depart out of thy mouth; but thou shalt meditate therein day and night, that thou mayest observe to do according to all that is written therein: for then thou shalt make thy way prosperous, and then thou shalt have good success. Have not I commanded thee? Be strong and of a good courage; be not afraid, neither be thou dismayed: for the LORD thy God is with thee whithersoever thou goest.*"[5]

Then and now courageous vision has always been based on the Word of God. And God measures this courage to us that we may cast vision in an America and in a world that operate in the twilight zone.

A voice and judge of the people, Supreme Court Justice Antonin Scalia, was quoted by *U.S. News and World Report* in their April 22, 1996, broadcast remarking that "**devout Christians are destined to be regarded as fools in modern society.**" We are living in a day when we are considered fools just for believing the Book, much less for having a courageous vision based on the Book. And when a devout Christian dares to cast vision, watch out because it is at that time the world grows furious or simply labels that work "extreme" or, worse, "cultish." Let the gainsayers question and let them doubt; let them throw discouraging words. There's a living God in Heaven, and His Spirit guides us as we catch His Word in our hearts and cast it out with our hands.

Biblical vision is clear, compassionate and courageous. It dares in a society that hates sold-out Christianity to determine that *we are going to be a very present help in a time of trouble in our country and in our world. We will make a difference, and that difference is our faith, and that faith is our victory.*

Of course we cannot pursue this alone because that is not God's plan. The strength of the church is not measured in the scope of the pastor's vision but in the commitment of the people in the pews to the Book. Courageous vision comes from people who share common beliefs and convictions, who pursue a God-given understanding of their role in their community. This understanding is based on their persuasion that the Book is **truth**, that God is in fact God, that God is through the leadership of His undershepherd communicating to them His desire for their involvement together with Him as colaborers in reaching their community and their world for Christ.

When the Apple Computer Corporation began its swift decline into near death in the early eighties, Steven P. Jobs, chairman of the board and chief stockholder, traveled from California's Silicon Valley to New York City to meet the Pepsi Company's John Sculley. The two met in Sculley's office, which overlooked the impressive

Manhattan skyline. Sculley firmly declined Jobs' offer to become the Apple president and chief marketing strategist unless Jobs would promise him one million in salary, one million in bonus and one million in severance regardless of the outcome of a joint endeavor.

Flabbergasted, Jobs gulped but agreed if Sculley would relocate to California. However, Sculley would only commit to a consulting position from New York. At that, Jobs issued a challenge to Sculley: "Do you want to spend the rest of your life selling sugared water, or do you want to change the world?"

In his autobiography, Sculley remembers that Jobs' challenge knocked the wind out of him. He admitted that he had become so caught up with the future of Pepsi, his pension and whether his family could adapt to life in California that an opportunity to change the world nearly passed him by. Instead, he gained perspective, and he and his family moved to California. They settled in just fine, and Sculley has not doubted the decision he made in an office overlooking Manhattan fifteen years ago.

And now I'll draw a parallel. God has given to His servants an opportunity to change the world, to turn it upside down, in fact. And the change agent is the Word of God cast before people, practically applied and modeled before them by Christians who love lost people enough not to stand by while they perish. So ask yourself this question: Are you going to change your world, or will you become overly concerned with the sugared water of your own manufacturing? **Don't substitute dangerous preoccupation with activities that are eternally insignificant for capitalizing on your spiritual opportunities.**

The church is asleep tonight. The church is in dormancy tonight. Do you remember David's trip to Israel's hideout as they cowered before the giant Goliath? Remember that **the definition of *vision* is "scriptural**

understanding." While people are carelessly cursing our God and belittling our faith, we are doing what David's older brother Eliab did—**NOTHING.** David heard the provocations of the giant, approached his brothers and asked, "Is there not a cause? Isn't there something at stake here? The name of our God is being blasphemed. Why isn't somebody doing something about it?"

The Bible records that David went before King Saul and **displayed his willingness** to meet the giant in the valley below, offering this boast, "I'll take care of this giant for you." They laughed at him. But notice that David's boast was not in himself. It was in the Lord. And yet they lightly esteemed the small stature of the young man before them and his apparent inability to lift Saul's armor, let alone overcome the giant.

Our secular peers will laugh and disdain our efforts to cast Biblical vision, and the entertainment industry openly mocks our calling. Saul's advisors amused themselves at David's expense, asking, "And how exactly do you think you will accomplish such a feat, young man?"

David responded, "Well I remember a day when a bear attacked my flock and another time when a lion stealthily approached my lambs, and my God, the Lord of all Israel, delivered me out of the mouth of the bear and out of the claws of the lion. He will deliver me from the likes of this giant too." Where did such a little guy get such a big faith? David had **developed that vision** in the wilderness while caring for the sheep. Convictions had been formed about the character of his God, which became the foundation of a courageous vision.

When David returned to his brother's anxious looks, Eliab turned an angry scowl toward David. And we can expect that **when we determine to realize a spiritual vision**, most people won't applaud, and many will caustically accuse us of pride or questionable motives in an effort to belittle our dreams. Sometimes it is people, and at other times it is the accuser of the brethren himself— Satan. It is interesting to note that Goliath's name means "the exiled one." Who else in the Scriptures was exiled? Lucifer, the angel of light, is the exiled one who lies in wait like David's lion did in search of undershepherds and their sheep.

When David received Eliab's scathing remarks, he didn't whine, "Oh, well, then, I had better get back to my sheep." No, he thought, *I've got to get down to the river and get me some rocks. I've got something to do. I've got a giant to fell.* He did not allow criticism to bind him. He understood the **definition** of *vision*. He had faithfully served among his sheep **developing** that vision. He had **displayed** courage in approaching the fulfillment of that vision. And now he was **determined** to accomplish that vision.

Every day Christopher Columbus wrote in a personal journal. Some of those entries are only four words— "Today we sailed on." We too will experience many days during the course of our spiritual journey when all we can record is "Today I sailed on." Be encouraged—sailing on is better than turning around. The implementation of spiritual vision is an act of obedience to God's Word, and sometimes that means we must stay the course without seeing visible results. This is the nature of vision. William Carey, recognized as the father of modern missions, called it plodding.

Another missionary, Hudson Taylor, pioneer to inland China, was criticized by others because of his creative ministry methods. He dressed like a Chinese man in an effort to be culturally relevant. He became the punch line of many leadership jokes; however, Hudson led thousands of Chinese to Christ despite the little imagination and littler faith of his peers. He pursued the vision God had given him, remarking, "Say what you want to say. These people need the Lord, and I'm going to lead them to Jesus any way God leads me."

Our family first gathered with our church in 1986 with a handful of people, each one committing himself to "look toward Heaven" at our commissioning service. I was a twenty-four-year-old pastor casting a vision before people with whom I shared common beliefs and convictions, but nobody took note of that. Between then and now, our vision has served over ten thousand people who have received Christ as their personal Saviour throughout our community and in surrounding cities. Each one of those decisions in God's eyes is a major victory, and those victories are the birth child of vision.

The man of God prays to God, gets a Biblical vision from God, stands up to proclaim the Word of God and is not hindered when trouble arrives. What would it take to interrupt your pursuit of God's vision? An older brother doubting your character? A family member questioning your motives and how your intentions may affect the family? A peer doubting your method? A situation unanticipated? A dream not realized exactly as you have hoped? Every spiritual vision is confronted with questions and counterfeit options that can distract the leader from experiencing **the destiny of the vision.** But within the context of God's vision is the safest place for the spiritual leader to serve.

Consider David again. David never envisioned being king. This is such an important observation. In the training seminars you attend and in the periodicals you read, they'll promote a philosophy that promises, "Set your sights on where you want to go, and you can do it because you're a good person. Go get 'em, tiger!" David never wanted to be a king. He wanted to be a good shepherd. He desired to obey his God and honor His name. God delights in molding people who are just trying to be good Christians into great instruments for His glory.

True spiritual vision brings us closer to God's destiny for our lives.

D. L. Moody once encouraged, "If God be your partner, make your plans large." And so we pray that God will help us to have convictions that are stronger than our fears, vision that is clearer than our doubts and a spiritual dissatisfaction that overpowers the status quo. May God help us to have poise more unshakable than panic, a desire to see people saved more than people appeased, and a courageous vision, because where there is no vision, people perish.

CHAPTER 10

Harvesting the Fruit

To serve the present age,
My calling to fulfill—
O may it all my pow'rs engage
To do my Master's will![1]

It is only as we develop others around us that we permanently succeed in the ministry. Maturing believers require a balance between their increasing faith and the function of that faith in practical ministry. Because of this, we realize that our core values are not kudos, a means of congratulating ourselves for a close walk with God, but a beginning place from which we are able first to recognize and then develop other servant leaders. A local church pastor who believes that his only responsibility is to teach the Bible has not captured the full understanding of his calling.

Paul addressed the privilege of discipleship, reminding leaders of the dual purpose of Christ's ascension, namely, to lead captivity captive and to give gifts to men. "He gave some, apostles; and some, prophets; and some, evangelists; and some, pastors and teachers; **For the perfecting of the saints, for the work of the ministry, for the edifying of the body of Christ.**"[2]

A colaborer in the ministry recently shared that she remembered the moment when she first realized that she should begin to minister to and help others. For two years she had grown in faith and knowledge in the Lord. She was an active member of her local church and a careful lay student of the Word, and yet she and many others still considered her as "the baby" of the family, although her steady growth was both promising and a joy to watch. One night she went to dinner with another young woman from the congregation. As they were talking, her guest began to ask her many questions about the Christian life in general, about the Bible and about the church. As the discussion continued, the young woman realized that for the first time in her Christian experience she was teaching someone else instead of having someone else teach her. Yes, it was in the informal setting of a restaurant. However, she has marked that moment as the time when she realized she had a responsibility before the Lord to begin sharing with others all that the Lord had been doing in her own life, and she did begin doing just that.

A little more than five years have passed since then; and with much encouragement and many godly, committed examples available to her, she has gained experience as a Sunday school teacher, summer camp counselor, choir member and witness. She has earned a bachelor's degree in Biblical studies and is now preparing to begin a full-time missions ministry.

There are men and women of all ages and backgrounds in churches across America who are similarly being challenged in their personal walk with Christ to express that which the Lord has impressed on their hearts through His Word. It is the responsibility and the privilege of spiritual leaders, first, to recognize these individuals through prayer; second, to share with them the "things that [they have] heard [from their own teachers and mentors] among many witnesses, [and to] commit [those things] to faithful men, who shall be able to teach others also."[3]

Most Christians realize the mission of the church is to evangelize the world with the Gospel of Christ, but a definite strategy of accomplishing this goal is often not clearly implemented. I am convinced that there exist large numbers of godly men and women in churches today who want to be used of God, who will gladly subscribe to the doctrines and leadership requirements of the church. Unfortunately, they are hindered by inefficient or nonexistent strategies designed to help them discover and develop their gifts and spiritual life for the work of the ministry, the edification and growth of the church.

We must focus on obstetrics *and* pediatrics. We focus on birthing lambs and forget the needs of maturing sheep, but we need a mature sheep to birth a lamb. Our philosophies and practice, or lack thereof, become our own worst enemy, defeating the purpose of our evangelism efforts. Only people who have been ministered to and developed in the Faith can minister to and develop others.

I often speak in churches across our country. Repeatedly the bulletins bulge with pleas for teachers, youth leaders, etc. It is difficult to view such influential positions as a "tag, you're it" type service. There may be areas of ministry for which the volunteer method is appropriate; however, spiritual leaders who prayerfully and practically recognize those among the congregation whom God is preparing for a ministry of leadership should also exercise a philosophy for developing these disciples.

I have chosen to use a detailed questionnaire as a tool to discern the commitment and to encourage potential full-time staff members in an interview setting. The time we spend together fosters openness for us to pray, for them to ask questions, express concerns and seek counsel if necessary.

Much prayer and time are invested in the process of recognizing and approaching members for recruitment to the staff leadership team. For instance, we often speak, preach, teach and model ways in which people may become a witness to lost people and share their faith in Christ. However, we very rarely hear mention of the fact that Christians can be witnesses to other Christians also—witnesses of that more abundant life marked by commitment and worship in spirit and service.

Those who join the local church leadership team should be witnesses of the Christ-centered life before the whole congregation. They should model attributes of godliness before they have opportunity to influence God's people in a leadership role. This is not a worldly type of performance-based acceptance, where people must perform before they are loved and accepted in the fellowship. Everyone is loved and appreciated in the fellowship of believers, but not everyone will exercise his spiritual gift(s) in a leadership role. Yes, we understand these believers are only human. It is the fact that they are human that causes their influence in the local church to be so potent.

The word *influence* is derived from the Latin word for *influenza* or what we commonly refer to today as the flu. How is the flu contracted? It is passed from person to person through one-on-one contact. Influence passes from person to person in a similar way—unseen. Instead of catching a head- and stomachache and a longing for the nearest Pepto-Bismol bottle, believers who are under the influence of a committed witness will long for a more meaningful Christian experience. They will become dissatisfied with their baby diet of milk (or, in this case, 7-Up and soda crackers) and long for the meat of the Word of God. The influence, positive or negative, of our leaders will significantly affect what the people catch from them, both inside and outside of the church house, whether it is spiritual life and growth or spiritual regression and apathy. As Dr. Lee Roberson is so often noted for saying, "Everything rises or falls on leadership."

A few times each month I receive a form in the mail asking me to evaluate a candidate for some position in our community as a deputy sheriff or an aerospace or social service worker. I appreciate these background checks. It amazes me that people will undergo tests, evaluations and interviews if a paycheck is involved. However, if a Christian ministry is cautious in their selection process, a cry is raised against "organized religion" and the label of legalism pasted over the sincere efforts of a pastor whose desire is to protect his flock. The Bible gives a mandate to the church to be patient before endorsing someone as a leader in the church. First Timothy 5:22 warns, "Lay hands suddenly on no man." A time of proving is both appropriate and Biblical.

An early illustration of leaders' recognizing other spiritual leaders occurs in Acts 6:3–5 when deacons are selected at the church in Jerusalem. They are men from among the congregation "of honest report, full of the Holy Ghost and wisdom" whom the apostles could appoint over certain aspects of the ministry. In this short yet suggestive passage of Scripture definite Biblical conclusions can be drawn regarding the selection of servant leaders. Note:

> **The principle of influence:** The fact that these men were found **among** the members of the congregation indicates that the people knew them and acknowledged their faithfulness. They exerted godly influence. While the apostles were capable and had authority to delegate assignments, they could not delegate influence. Godly influence is something the Holy Spirit of God develops only through yielded vessels.

> **The principle of credibility:** These were men of **honest report**. They exercised integrity worthy of leadership. Their character reflected God's character. They "fleshed-out" faithfulness. "The apostles knew that they would only make the problem

worse if they delegated this task to men who had questionable reputations."[4]

The principle of spirituality: These were men filled or controlled by God's Spirit, daily exercising the fruits of His Spirit. Additionally, I believe that God's grace manifests itself in the life of a Spirit-filled Christian by enabling him to resolve in a Christ-honoring way what has the potential to be an explosive and divisive issue. A carnal Christian always makes a small problem bigger, but a spiritual Christian always makes a big problem smaller. Related to and probably in part because of this, a spiritual leader is enabled to glorify Christ through his life and testimony.

The principle of wisdom: The men were **full of wisdom.** Wisdom is vital to the life and health of the church body, and the source of that wisdom is Christ and His Word. The first chapter of Joshua, verse 7, tells us that God called Joshua to a specific leadership task. He commanded him, *"Be thou strong and very courageous, that thou mayest observe to do according to all the law, which Moses my servant commanded thee: **turn not from it to the right hand or to the left, that thou mayest prosper whithersoever thou goest.**"* Likewise, the Proverbs clearly show a contrast between the simple and the wise man. Without wisdom there will be a lack of direction and the tendency to major on minors and minor on majors. Lee Iacoca once said, "Even the right decision is the wrong decision if it is made too late." We need men of wisdom who will make the right decisions at the right time.

The principle of humble service: The first deacons were men committed to the task of serving others, following after Christ, and ministering according to the "appointments" or direction of the apostles. The fact is that every godly leader must recognize that he is under authority as he renders service in the ministry. We must do the work God has called us to do in humility as unto the Lord. Great leaders are not as interested in fighting for a position as they are in solving problems. In many cases their presence and example are the solution itself.

The principle of active faith: Acts 6:5 tells us that Stephen was **full of faith.** We need men and women serving in the church today who still believe that He "is able to do exceeding abundantly above all that we ask or think."[5] Periodically I will meet a pastor or deacon or teacher who feels he is "called" to question every spiritual endeavor of the ministry, whether the task is to purchase a vehicle, build a building or support a missionary. For some reason certain people feel it is spiritual to be the one negative voice on every issue. While there is nothing wrong with someone's having a differing opinion (and sometimes in the right spirit this can be helpful), it is certainly not a sign of spirituality to question each step of faith taking place in the ministry. I believe the Holy Spirit of God desires that each local church should "stand fast in one spirit, with one mind striving together for the faith of the gospel."[6] It is time that attitude determines action. Today more than ever we need leaders with an attitude of faith.

Although recognizing leaders is an important first step in developing them, it is incomplete without mentoring. It is vital that those who are currently in leadership of the local church spend time with and mentor the future ministry leaders. Jesus took a small band of unlikely candidates, and by allowing them time with Himself, He developed them into a world-changing group of preachers. I cannot emphasize enough the importance of spending quality time in fellowship, prayer and ministry with your leaders-in-training. A leader can *impress* people from a distance, but his *impact* is felt up close through one-on-one fellowship and discipleship.

Over the years my wife, Terrie, and I have entertained hundreds of young Christians in our home. In the comfort of our family circle we have shared our thoughts and experiences in the Christian life with a new believer in search of a mentor, a model of faith and a friend. I like to think of these times as spiritual pediatrics, when future leaders are inoculated from the potential fiery darts of the Devil. In this setting we are also able to identify areas of vulnerability and need in the believer's life.

At a pastors' conference some years ago I heard a lecture that discouraged pastors from spending too much time with their people. The speaker especially warned against inviting people into one's home. The message further stressed the need to develop a personal "mystique." At the time, the concept of having my very own mystique and keeping a distance from people seemed like the best way to maintain closeness to God. However, I have come to the conviction that men with such a philosophy are making a "mystique mistake." First, if we ever attain some type of mystique, let it be from the Holy Spirit of God. Second, we will never truly mentor people in the ways of God until we identify personally with them. Consider a passage of Scripture from the Second Epistle to the Corinthians. Paul confides,

> *"And such trust have we through Christ to God-ward: Not that we are sufficient of ourselves to think any thing as of ourselves; but our sufficiency is of God; Who also hath made us able ministers of the new testament; not of the letter, but of the spirit: for the letter killeth, but the spirit giveth life. But if the ministration of death, written and engraven in stones, was glorious, so that the children of Israel could not stedfastly behold the face of Moses for the glory of his countenance; which glory was to be done away: How shall not the ministration of the spirit be rather glorious?"*

> *"Seeing then that we have such hope, we use great plainness of speech: And not as Moses, which put a vail over his face, that the*

children of Israel could not stedfastly look to the end of that which is abolished."[7]

Although there is much to be gleaned from this passage of Scripture, a comparison is stated: Moses hid his face from the children of Israel by necessity. Jesus lived with His disciples and invited three into the Mount of Transfiguration with Him. Whereas God met with Moses alone under the old covenant, now God's Spirit indwells all believers.

"Now the Lord is that Spirit: and where the Spirit of the Lord is, there is liberty. But we all, with open face beholding as in a glass the glory of the Lord, are changed into the same image from glory to glory, even as by the Spirit of the Lord."[8]

God is looking for people who, like Christ, will give Him their lives for the redemption of men—lives spent training leaders to follow Him. Please remember that the salutation of the Book of Acts announces, *"The former treatise have I made, O Theophilus, of all that **Jesus began both to do and teach."** Further study in this explosive book charting the history of the early church reveals that what Jesus began to do and teach the disciples during His earthly ministry, He continued to do and teach through His disciples after Pentecost. We also should carry the mantle, by the ability that the Spirit of Christ gives, doing those things that Jesus would do and teaching those things that Jesus taught before our churches and in the company of our disciples in particular.

Now I do believe that it is unwise to spend large chunks of time with one friend or one couple to the exclusion of others. Godly fellowship has guidelines. We must be approachable and available to the leaders that God would have us develop—those whom God has helped us to recognize through prayer and to begin developing in practical ways, such as men's leadership meetings, women's fellowships, prayer meetings, leadership retreats, discipleship programs, deacon orientation, home fellowships and Bible studies.

Over the years I have encouraged the leaders of our ministry to remember to have **fellowship with a purpose.** I believe Jesus had a purpose in mind as He fellowshiped with the disciples. Too often the fellowship in our churches today is self-centered rather than Christ-centered. It is my prayer that by identifying with the Lord first through my walk with Him and then through fellowship with His people, I can influence others to know Jesus and the joy of a committed life in His service. I can demonstrate that real Christianity is distinct from the pagan culture around us and teach that integrity begins in our personal lives with an intimate relationship with God. I am also able to comfort them with the promise that fellow Christians are praying for them and available to them beginning with me, and I encourage them to believe that God is able to do great things through surrendered people.

I thank God for a handful of men who have identified with me in mentoring. No, they never announced themselves as mentors; they simply came alongside of me to spend time with me and nurture me in my faith. These men have never uttered an off-color joke. They have always been patient and generous. Their concern for me has been humbling. Only God knows the difference they have made in my life.

As I consider the investment such men have made in my own life, I am motivated to make similar investments in those I recognize and mentor in the Faith. However, mentoring is not an end in itself. The process must proceed to the next step which is equipping. Equipping is not dumping jobs onto available bodies. Christians seeking meaningful involvement appreciate training materials and sessions. We equip future leaders with skills in these areas, appreciating that it is God who gives them the ability to exercise their spiritual gifts in a leadership capacity.

God has placed the seed of faith in their hearts. His Spirit indwells them. His gift for the purpose of His glory is bestowed for the edification of the body. We may water the seed, but we did not create the seed, which bears the fruit of God's will. We are workers together with God, husbandmen in His field, participating in His harvest of disciples. Therefore, let us complement our prayers to the Lord of the harvest to send forth more laborers with a commitment to equip those laborers for the task.

Many leaders fail to take a necessary next step and delegate the task to the person they have equipped for that task. It seems we don't mind mentoring and equipping, but we struggle to share the ministry with others. Unfortunately, if people are not allowed the opportunity to share in the real ministry, they are hindered in exercising a leadership role, and the entire organization is stifled. Maturity doesn't come with age. It comes with acceptance of responsibility. The only way that discernment is developed is by placing leaders in decision-making roles, even if they are wrong from time to time.

Recently I had the joy of taking my family with me to a Bible conference where I was preaching in Las Vegas, Nevada. As we traveled to the meeting I asked our daughter Danielle if she would like to drive. Mind you, as a 17-year-old, she had already been through the steps of recognition, mentoring and equipping. In fact, she has the driver's license to prove it! The truth, however, is that the only way she will ever develop safe driving skills is by our delegating more responsibility to her in the area of driving.

As Danielle took the wheel, I could feel the tension mount. For the first time in our family history, I was in the back seat having delegated the responsibility of driving to Danielle. Overall she did a great job of driving. She also learned the priority of staying out of the fast lane when eighteen-wheelers want to pass. Delegating that responsibility to Danielle was awkward for me but necessary for her. The same is true in the delegation of ministry.

When I was first called to pastor the Lancaster Baptist Church, there were twelve voting members who unanimously invited us to come to the church. Of course there would be no salary or moving expenses paid, but there was an opportunity to reach a community for Christ. At that time I became the pastor, teacher, Sunday school director, youth pastor, choir leader, counselor—you get the picture. Today there are hundreds of lay leaders and a team of pastors who lead a wonderful staff of dedicated believers, and the community is being reached. It has not always been easy to delegate various responsibilities, but as God has provided men and women to lead, our shared ministry responsibilities have proven effective.

Why do we often hesitate to delegate and share in the ministry? Several reasons have surfaced over the years and are revealed in these common questions that other pastors have asked me. Perhaps the answer I supply will further encourage you to share the responsibility.

What if they don't do as good a job as I've done with it?
They may not at first, but give them time and training, and they may exceed your expectations. Turn your anxiety into anticipation for their success and Christian maturity.

What if the people like the way he conducts the meeting better than the way I do it?
Praise the Lord! So long as he is faithful to the Word and the philosophy of the ministry, be willing to share the joy of serving.

What if he is rejected or yelled at for the way he leads a ministry?

Use this as an opportunity to coach him if he
made a mistake and encourage him if he didn't.
Nobody said ministry is easy.

What if no one wants to share the responsibility?
Model before them a joy in serving and invite
them to help. God will touch the right person's heart.

There are two basic reasons why we do not delegate
as we could and should. The first reason is insecurity
related to a lack of spiritual growth in the grace of the
Lord, which we studied in Chapter 2. Even worse, we
may be seeking an inordinate amount of gratification
(fleshly ego) from people rather than finding our acceptance in the Lord. This is a real challenge for younger
pastors, but unfortunately many pastors of tenure have
yet to win the battle of insecurity. The second major reason we do not delegate is that we are disorganized. We
have no process, no strategy, that allows for leadership
development. I have outlined the process of delegation
in the following way:

1. Remember to mentor and teach before delegation.
2. Give clearly identifiable duties for the given task.
3. Verbalize confidence in the person to whom you
   delegate.
4. Give him authority to get the job done.
5. Establish budget limits if applicable.
6. Allow him room to fail and learn from his mistakes.
7. Set predetermined checkpoints for evaluation.
8. Praise him and give him credit for a job well done.

The seventh item on our list mentions evaluation, a
form of accountability. Accountability is sharing goals
in a measurable way formally or informally. Accountability to and responsibility for one another are both
appreciated and needed in the church family, especially
among the leadership team. Withholding Biblical and

consistent evaluation from our disciples is a form of spiritual robbery. Without positive, tough, loving accountability, those we invest in are hindered in their spiritual development.

One author draws an excellent analogy between the church family and our physical families. She affirms that "physical families have tough love. It's because they care so desperately about how each other turns out. They are so closely bound together that [each one's] success is the others' status, and [each one's] failure is the others' pain....I believe God is going to help His spiritual family to be close enough to care enough—to identify enough to have enough tough love!"[9]

Growing leaders need to be challenged, and they need to communicate with other team players. In the context of leadership, delegating a task and not following up is a proven formula that equals frustration and lack of productivity. After several informal and/or formal meetings of review and a season of time, our disciples will acquire zeal and skill in the ministry. Those activities which were sown in patience, praying, mentoring, equipping, delegating and evaluating will bear a harvest of joyful and effective service.

The bearing of fruit is both a physical reality and a spiritual allegory. An interesting verse in the first chapter of Genesis reveals that God created the earth to "bring forth grass, the herb yielding seed, and the fruit tree yielding fruit after his kind, **whose seed is in itself.**"[10] Might I suggest that just as the fruits of the earth have the seeds of multiplication within themselves, likewise the Spirit of Christ indwelling our disciples is the seed of spiritual multiplication that inhabits their hearts. The investment we make in their lives is living water flowing out from us, and the Word of God is that light which produces the photosynthesis causing that seed of faith to grow and multiply itself.

As the local church matures in its understanding of the global mandate for gospel propagation, God will also call leaders out from our congregations and give our church families the responsibility of sending them out to multiply the testimony of Christ according to the Biblical pattern indicated in Acts 13. The leading men at Antioch had been ministering to the Lord, praying and fasting, when the Spirit commanded, "Separate me Barnabus and Saul for the work whereunto I have called them."[11] Despite the loss of qualified leadership in their own congregation, by faith they sacrificed their men to minister elsewhere, sending them with their blessing and support.

Take note of the holy process of multiplication that is evidenced in this passage. These men were not looking for a career change. They were actively seeking God. God desires that we send forth laborers into His harvest field, and the church is the sending agent.

In addition, I want to share my conviction that it is imperative that church leaders begin to involve teenagers in their strategy of leadership development. We must challenge them with the opportunity of giving their lives to God's ministry. Let us pray that the Holy Spirit would call many of them to His service. One of the best services we have each year in our church is the "Youth Night Service." On this night, the teenagers lead the singing, make the announcements and preach. There is something wrong in our churches when teens think the ministry is a last-resort option. We should pray God will use our testimonies to encourage people in our churches with the potential of a life invested in the ministry.

A few years ago the Lord began to burden my heart greatly for the city of Los Angeles. Los Angeles is a city of over three million people with relatively few gospel-preaching churches. After months of prayer, we secured a meeting place at the Belmont High School and organized groups for our church to canvass the surrounding neighborhoods with gospel invitations.

As we head into the twenty-first century, the Los Angeles Baptist Church is officially chartered, and the pastor is a man trained through our ministry. This is truly a multiplication of ministry! I believe the development of the new pastor's life through the Word of God and the local church has equipped him to make a difference in the needy city of Los Angeles.

All Christians, young and old, have a God-given purpose and calling in life to influence their world for Christ. And so we should respond with joy when the Holy Spirit leads our church to multiply. We should be willing lovingly and sacrificially to support the expansion of Christ's ministry in the next town or foreign country.

Finally, I believe the entire process of leadership development must be saturated in prayer. From the beginning phase of recognition through the processes of mentoring, equipping, delegating, evaluating and multiplying, we must pray to the Lord of the harvest for the emerging spiritual leader, his protection and provision. We must pray for the anointing of God upon that life as he does the will of God from his heart.

In order to see change, in order to see spiritual revival, we must have more than a well-laid strategy; we must have the touch of God upon our lives. We are unable to develop effective programs of leadership development apart from a commitment to support those in leadership with our own prayers. John 15:5 says it best: "I am the vine, ye are the branches: He that abideth in me, and I in him, the same bringeth forth much fruit: for without me ye can do nothing." Abiding in Christ alone we are enabled to tap into His power which effectively works in us and through us to accomplish His purposes in the ministry.

Paul set a Biblical standard in praying for those to whom he ministered, and we may notice also that those whom Paul trained continued in his steps, praying for those to whom they ministered. Consider Epaphras. Although we cannot be dogmatic about the details of his spiritual development, the Scriptures do give us some clues. Epaphras was influenced directly or indirectly through the ministry of Paul in Ephesus. Paul had spent three full years ministering in Ephesus working alongside Priscilla and Aquila, whom he had met in Corinth and had developed in the Faith. The testimony of Christ by this leadership team in Ephesus traveled a hundred miles east and was proclaimed in Colosse by Epaphras who played a major role in the evangelism and growth of the Colossian church body.

Years later, during his imprisonment, Paul wrote a letter to the Colossians whom he had never met. He assured them of his own prayers and how he always gave "thanks to God...the Father of our Lord Jesus Christ, praying always for [them]."[12] He also revealed the incredible prayer life of his disciple and fellow prisoner, Epaphras, who labored "fervently for [them] in prayers, that [they might] stand perfect and complete in all the will of God." Paul continued bearing record that Epaphras had a great zeal for them and for those in Laodicea and Hierapolis.[13] This man held three cities before the Lord in consistent, intercessory, compassionate prayer. Let us live and do likewise. The legacy of our prayer lives doesn't end with us. It is reproduced in the lives of those we love and disciple.

Leadership development is never an event or a destination. Successful ministries have discovered that leadership development is a life process. As spiritual leaders, we must create an environment where training is accessible at all times and at all levels. As the gifts of our people mature, we must continue promoting them, allowing them to rise to their personal calling. We must center our hope and strategy in the Lord, knowing that He is the One who gives the increase. No one has ever mastered the art of leading people except the Master Himself, who is more than an example of how to live and lead. He is life itself.

We will always have more to learn, experience and consider as we form and apply Biblical strategies for leadership development. Let us be encouraged as we continue harvesting souls and disciples in the fields of the Lord. His Word still beckons, "Take my yoke upon you, and learn of me; for I am meek and lowly in heart: and ye shall find rest unto your souls. For my yoke is easy, and my burden is light." [14]

Section 5

Making a Difference

CHAPTER 11

Banyan Trees and Building Teams

I think that I shall never see
A poem lovely as a tree—

....

A tree that looks at God all day,
And lifts her leafy arms to pray;

....

Poems are made by fools like me,
But only God can make a tree.[1]

I believe that God's desire for His people, and specifically for local churches, is that with one spirit and one mind we should work together for the Faith of the Gospel. We could say **that God's desire is that we grow together.** Paul encouraged the Philippians to grow together, and I find it particularly interesting to note that the theme of the letter in which this instruction appears is joy—joy in serving, joy in that the good work which God has begun in us He will complete, joy in that we may learn how to approve things that are excellent sincerely and without offense, joy in being like-minded and loving one another, joy in humility, joy in difficult circumstances of suffering, joy in the proclaiming of the Gospel, joy in the sacrifice and service of faith, joy in knowing God, joy in all things.

But let us not confuse joy with happiness. The motto of a leadership team in ministry is *not* "Don't worry; be happy." Our churches are part of God's household, a family of believers coming together for edification, discipline and growth. We pray together and we serve together as an expression of our love for our Bridegroom and soon-coming King. Our services are not a form of escapism. Rather, they are a time to bear one another's burdens and to rejoice in the unfailing promises of the God who has called us out of this world. Therefore, our goals are holiness and love for the brethren, which produce a true joy that is far better than circumstantial happiness.

Is growing, and specifically growing together in this way, hard? Is change often difficult? And why must the outcome of our striving be *change* when our faith and our God are *unchanging?* The answer: we are called to be disciples. The definition of a *disciple* is one who learns, and *learning is transfiguration.* Yes, growing is hard and change is difficult. Its purpose is that as God's people, we should grow into Christlikeness, obediently serving from the heart with pure motives and, yes, joy. One man has expressed the frustrations of growth in this way:

> This plant would like to grow
> And yet be embryo;
> Increase, and yet escape
> The doom of taking shape.[2]

Have you ever heard of or seen a banyan tree? It is a plant of God's creation that has the ability to teach a specific spiritual lesson. The banyan tree, which is indigenous to East India and found in many tropical climates, begins as a single tree with a single trunk. As it grows it sends out shoots (or aerial roots) that plunge down into the soil. These take root to form secondary trunks. Eventually one tree produces a great forest in which it is impossible to tell the original trunk. A mature banyan almost gives the appearance of a large tree with very long shaggy-haired branches reaching to the ground in a tangled mass.

The largest tree of this kind in the world is found in

Hawaii on the island of Maui. One tree populates five miles of land. Although it is indeed an amazing tree, the spiritual lesson it communicates is more significant. As we grow, our roots should grow deeper into the foundation which is Christ. And from us branches of faith must shoot forth, growing down into the soil of other hearts, taking root in order that through our own growth in grace, other servant leaders are formed. Over time a fertile forest of disciple leaders is found to be rooted and grounded in Christ.

The ministry of a leader, then, will be similar to that of a man of forestry. His occupation is to care for, develop and cultivate forests. However, this man is never concerned that the trees will stop growing in his absence. The thought is absurd. Likewise, Paul expressed his confidence in the Philippian believers that whether he was present or absent from them, they would continue to strive together for the Faith of the Gospel. This confidence is the same confidence of all team-building pastors. Even in their absence, the Word is still preached; the ministry continues.

Yes, there is much we can learn from a tree because just as the Bible points to the Creator to explain creation, creation points back to the Creator and illustrates Biblical truth. Consider Psalm 92:12, 13: "The righteous shall flourish like the palm tree: he shall grow like a cedar in Lebanon. Those that be planted in the house of the LORD shall flourish in the courts of our God."

A common dictionary definition of *flourish* is "to grow luxuriantly: to reach a height of development or influence." Here is a well-known verse: "The fruit of the righteous is a tree of life; and he that winneth souls is wise."[3] Or compare the wicked, which have no root or branch, to the righteous, whose root shall yield fruit and never be moved. Even our Lord was referred to prophetically as a Branch that would grow out of the root of Jesse.

169

Do you see a scriptural pattern forming? The point is that the mascot of our ministries is not an unmoving stump. We are to grow. We must branch out into others' lives. Only then will we see the Gospel of grace take root in other hearts and yield fruit.

Can you imagine the work involved if, God forbid, they tried to uproot the banyan tree of Maui, whose diameter extends five miles? A ministry dependent on one man alone is easily chopped down. A team ministry through encouragement, accountability and Biblical instruction is not easily uprooted.

Paul specifically rejoiced, addressing the Philippians as true yokefellow, and asked them to help those who had **labored with him** in the Gospel, whose names are written in the Book of Life. In fact, the Epistles are full of names mentioned by Paul, John, James and Peter of believers who made a difference by laboring together with the same mind and spirit for the furtherance of the Gospel. **None of these men stood alone in the ministry.**

You can be in a ministry of a hundred people and make a difference in this world and in your community. I am a firm believer that the size of the congregation has nothing to do with the impact of that congregation. No matter the length of our membership list, our attitude ought to be to develop a team that will lift up the name of Jesus and minister the Gospel of grace in our church and community.

Pastors must develop other leaders in the church, and these believers must be coalesced into a team that will win victories for God's glory, not unlike the practice of the apostles. Teamwork is not just a good idea—it is the Biblical pattern for ministry. In reality, it is the Holy Spirit of God who adds to the local church team such as should be added, but the pastor has a specific commission to nurture and develop that team for the glory of God that they may do the work of the ministry.

Leadership teams are born when God's people are inspired to develop a greater heart for God. All inspiration originates with God; and yet it is often communicated or channeled through spoken testimony, teaching, preaching and participation in worship, prayer and Christian service. This love for God is the root from which all effective and fruit-bearing ministry grows. Thus, we must not forget in staff meetings, teachers' meetings, deacons' meetings and other such gatherings to come back to this basic: a love relationship with God.

Just because someone is holding a position of leadership in ministry does not guarantee he has a love relationship with the Lord. Too many of us know from experience the tragedy of seeing a friend or mentor dishonor the Saviour. We wonder how and why and what next. Be assured that such things occur when a leader's heart is not in proper fellowship with God. Proverbs 4:23 warns us to "keep thy heart with all diligence; for out of it are the issues of life." It is vital that leaders hunger and thirst after righteousness. The love of Christ must constrain them, for the character of the teacher will produce the confidence of the learner. The compassion of the teacher will produce the learner's motivation. The teacher's content will produce the learner's perception.[4]

> So, the focus in teaching is primarily on what you as the teacher do, and the focus in learning is primarily on what the student does. But we test the effectiveness of your teaching not by what you do, but by what the student does as a result of what you do. The simplest definition I know for learning is this: Learning is change.[5]

You may be wondering: by what process will these students enroll to become disciple leaders? Initially, inclusion on the team may mean something as simple as church membership. Acts 2:41 states, "Then they that gladly received his word were baptized: and the same day there were added unto them about three thousand souls." It is important that we recognize the need for personal relationships with new members of the church.

Those seeking church membership often go through a four-phase process before they decide to join with a church family. First, there is the interfacing stage when the pastor or a staff member visits to discuss various aspects of the ministry. It is at this phase that one is first inspired to have a heart for God and subsequently invited upon his testimony of saving faith to place his membership with that body of believers.

After interfacing comes the matter of bonding. In today's culture, bonding may come weeks or even months after the first visit to a church. A church committed to developing godly relationships will enhance the bonding process with activities geared for different people groups within the church. At some point in the bonding process comes the stage of acceptance. This is when an individual not only feels accepted but also accepts those around him or her.

Once this phase is reached, a person often comes to a place of ownership. Ownership is the platform from which team members are selected and trained. Someone at the ownership stage expresses with his life and with his words, "I believe in this ministry, and I desire to be a part of the spiritual victories and development of God's people for His glory in the days ahead." As this occurs, the pastor must guide potential team members to realize their individual callings within the framework of the team. Borrowed callings, like borrowed beliefs, are not adequate foundations for teamwork.

The foundation which effective ministry teams are built upon is sound instruction from the Word of God. Paul commanded Timothy that he should commit to faithful believers the things he had learned with the result that they would be able to teach others also. The vehicle by which a pastor is able to commit the things he has learned to his people is Biblical preaching; however, the work of teaching may also be accomplished through the adult Bible class ministry and the personal discipleship courses of the local church.

Small Bible study and discipleship groups foster a coaching environment. The leader of the church sees firsthand the level of hunger a newly included member has for the Word and ministry of God.

> Coaches spend a great deal of time talking to their teams, telling them what and why things must be done. They review films, study play books, prepare game plans, then they go to the practice area and begin to apply the what and why. Ninety percent of coaching is the nitty-gritty of the gym or practice field. The question is, apart from 15 hours of preparing that sermon, how [should servant leaders spend their time?] A smart and responsible pastor also spends time making sure his teaching is applied, training people and providing vehicles for both training and ministry expression.[6]

The observation of leadership among an emerging team happens when the team members become involved in the ministry. Jesus led His disciples into situations where they would learn for themselves. These situations may at times have seemed spontaneous to the disciples, but they were well planned by the Master Teacher. We are not seeking warm bodies to fill vacancies in the ministry; we are investing ourselves in others that they might minister victoriously.

A few years ago a young adult man I know accepted Christ as his personal Saviour. His background revealed lethal addictions and gross immorality. However, his growth in the Word and the Christian disciplines was indeed beautiful and exciting. It appeared that the Lord was giving him victory over past strongholds in his life. After several months with us, he moved to another state. Of course we challenged him to find a Bible-preaching church and to continue in the grace and knowledge of God.

Some weeks passed, and I received a letter from this young man. I was happy to see that he had found a church, but I was shocked to hear that after two weeks at the church he had become the youth pastor. He wrote, "When they found out I was from Lancaster Baptist Church, they wanted me to work with the youth." Obviously, the church did not have a pattern for team building and may have jeopardized the young man's spiritual development, as well as those he would influence.

Of course involvement in ministry is in itself an important avenue for leadership development. The classroom alone has never been enough. There came a time in the mentoring relationship between Christ and His disciples when He sent them out to learn firsthand of the challenges and blessing of ministry. Matthew 10:1 states, "And when he had called unto him his twelve disciples, he gave them power against unclean spirits, to cast them out, and to heal all manner of sickness and all manner of disease." As Jesus sent the disciples out, they went out with clear instructions, and they returned for a time of evaluation and affirmation. This is why leadership meetings for training and also for evaluation are paramount in the equipping of disciples and the building of leadership teams. We might think of it as debriefing.

Every servant leader must first be a disciple of Christ. He must also be a disciple maker. This is ministry multiplied. This is how we will have an impact in our communities and in our world for Christ. Commit to team building. Commit to truth, for truth never fears a challenge. As we connect with others who are committed, we can change our world.

One of the great weaknesses to which Christians succumb is an attitude of criticism. Rather than a habit of intercession and a seeking after God's sufficiency and wisdom, we develop a critical spirit. In fact, we see this occurring all around us. Let me emphasize that I am not condoning compromise or ecumenism. This is a call to cooperation with those of like-minded faith. Tragically, we see good men within our own circles shooting at each other. Instead of embracing the ninety-nine percent they agree on, they find the one thing they would do a little bit differently.

Thank God for these godly men who have served and are serving their generation, but we need a new generation of fundamental leaders who will rise above such behavior. The only accomplishment of such divisiveness is harm to our own churches. A soldier once observed, "Friendly fire isn't friendly." A critical spirit equals ministry suicide. We don't need to be generating an attitude of, "Well, where did you go to school?" or "With whom do you side on a particular issue?" My Bible says that when we start saying, "I am of Paul" or "I am of Apollos," then we must examine ourselves. Aren't we acting carnally? God, deliver us from this carnality!

I predict that those who take this divisive approach to ministry will shrink in number, although they may go down screaming and kicking, gaining much notice. Such temper tantrums only hurt their own flocks as well as the testimony of fundamental Bible-believing churches everywhere. There needs to be a revival of a good attitude in our fundamental churches today.

Good attitude is critical to effective team building because the attitude of the flock is formed by the attitude of the pastor. What a pastor says from the pulpit, even in his announcements, affects the people's perspective and passion. Unfortunately, some pastors today have become experts in knowing what can't be done, and this negative attitude is often communicated to others in various ways. Henry Ford once announced, "I'm looking for a lot of men with an infinite capacity for not knowing what can't be done." These are the people that complement and create an effective team for God's glory. Pastors, beware. Actions of faith are learned, but the attitude which supports that faith is contagious. What are you passing on to your people?

Serving Christ is our calling and challenge, so let us commit to preaching the Gospel of our Saviour with an attitude of faith motivated by genuine and ever increasing belief, for one day we will give an account to Christ for our service. Remember: a negative attitude says more about one's belief, or lack thereof, in God than it does about the particular issue for which one lobbies inappropriately. We conform to the image of Christ, not the image others desire of us or the negative attitude that some model.

There is something truly exciting about working with a team of Christians under the guidance of the Holy Spirit in order to realize a destiny of Biblical victory. And there is no doubt that in this day of speedy change and spiritual apathy, it is possible to lead a team to spiritual victory. If we are truly going to make a difference through the local church ministry in the twenty-first century, leaders must determine to build teams of people who truly desire to serve for the glory of God.

Building a team requires time and commitment. It involves building relationships with the members of the team. Many church leaders get so caught up in administration and paperwork that they forget to invest in the lives of their people.

> All of us task-oriented, obsessive/compulsives must learn to slow down and let people into our lives. It may be popular in the '90s to be a fast tracker with a full DayTimer, but we will only

impact people spiritually and permanently by that one-on-one contact that can't be substituted. In this age of telecommunication and telecommuting, there is still no substitute for quiet prolonged exposure of one soul to another.[7]

Learn to enjoy teamwork. After all, anything worth doing is worth doing together. The goal of a leadership team is proclaimed in Psalm 34:3: "O magnify the LORD with me, and let us exalt his name together." Such an invitation to participate in the redemptive and remarkable work of God with a team of like-minded believers inspires me for the task of service.

> A team has as many resources as there are persons. An individual is limited to the skills of one. A principle in mathematics is called synergism. A synergism is simply a happening that takes place when the sum of the total equals more than the sum of the parts...something extra happens when a team works together....A team will see the possibilities of discipleship from more perspectives than an individual. A fellowship multiplies the outcome.[8]

Some pastors, while practicing a high work ethic, unconsciously harbor a low opinion of the necessity of fellowship—camaraderie. But fellowship is a tool in the continuing process of an equipping ministry. We are not going to develop a team without fellowship. We may not think we have time to take our staff to a ball game or invite them to our homes, but we don't have time not to. We need to redeem the time, and that includes building relationships.

Relationships foster acceptance, and acceptance is the optimal environment of change. Our activities with our staff members communicate an important message: "I love you. I'm glad we're on the team together." It doesn't always have to be an elaborate endeavor. We can have some pizza delivered to a deacons' meeting, or we can use other creative means to spend time connecting with our people. They are a part of us, and we are a part of them. We are a team. We are accountable to Christ and to one another. Through relationships we become connected to our people. We know how they are feeling—if there is a depression, a misunderstanding or a falling away, etc.

We need to invest more time in building relationships in the church than in solving problems. Relationships are often the solution to our problems.

Genuine relationships help us to escape the nagging fear and insecurity that the people involved in our difficult situations are acting with intentional malice. Through relationships, we'll have the advantage of knowing better than that. If we truly respect and believe in our people, then we need to take a moment to calm down and communicate with them. I have found it particularly helpful to begin with praise, lovingly correct them and then set goals to remedy the situation. It sounds something like this:

> I appreciate what you do on this staff, Dave. You have been so helpful in a particular area. Now recently you did something or acted in a certain way. In the future, this would be a better approach, and this is why. Do you have any questions or concerns about this? Thank you, Dave, for your time and commitment to this ministry. We really appreciate you.

With this emphasis upon building relationships, a caution must be voiced. Ministry, and especially a ministry that invites members and teams to build relationships, must have integrity as its guiding principle. This of course applies in both the moral and financial realms. Be advised to set up safeguards within the context of building those relationships. As ministers of the Gospel we are to be blameless. Of course, being blameless doesn't mean we will never be blamed, but we can exercise discernment in our daily interactions with the men and women of faith that we serve.

The Bible clearly expresses that women should seek the counsel of their husbands when they have questions, and they should. In cases requiring counsel that a husband is unable to give, the Bible also gives instruction: the older women are to teach the younger women, and in a like manner the older men are to teach the younger men. Protect yourself and guard your testimony. Our character is supposed to be a reflection of our God.

Let this not distract from the positive aspects of building relationships that keep our people from becoming a modern visual aid that screams, "Because I am not the hand, I am not of the body! Because I am not the eye, I am not of the body!" Do we have freedom to conclude differently than Paul did? God forbid. Rather, we agree that if the whole body were an eye, how would we hear? If the whole body were hearing, how would we smell?

"But now hath God set the members every one of them in the body, as it hath pleased him."

"But now are they many members, yet but one body. And the eye cannot say unto the hand, I have no need of thee: nor again the head to the feet, I have no need of you. Nay, much more those members of the body, which seem to be more feeble, are necessary."[9]

Few pastors would state so boldly that a staff member was unimportant or easily replaced, but sometimes we say exactly that without words when we disrespect our people or care so little that we refuse to build relationships with them or help them identify their gifts and calling. General Eisenhower once rebuked one of his generals for referring to a soldier as "just a private." He reminded him that the army could function better without its generals than it could without its foot soldiers. "If this war is won," he said, "it will be won by privates."

In the same way, the common, ordinary, one-gift

Christians are the very backbone of the church. We have our great evangelists, our large congregations led by dynamic leaders and our wealthy brethren who are able to finance great works. But if the work of the Lord is to be done and if the Gospel is to be taken to the lost, then it will be accomplished by *ordinary* Christians.

There is no such thing as a spiritual caste system. God has gifted every Christian, and each Christian and team member must understand his spiritual gift(s), exercising them within the framework of that team.

Fundamental pastors appear shy about teaching the spiritual gifts. We have allowed our insecurities about the charismatic movement to scare us from proclaiming what is true from the Word. Some of the gifts taught in the Scriptures were *temporary sign gifts* whose function ceased with the completion of the New Testament canon; however, the remaining gifts are *permanent edifying gifts,* and we must **teach about them and help our people to identify their own gift(s).** Our failure to do so hinders their development into the people God intends them to be.

The Greek word for *equip* is *katartizo.* Like many Greek words it is rich in meaning and has been used historically and Biblically in various contexts. John Hendrix and Lloyd Householder in their work entitled *The Equipping of Disciples* provide insight concerning the Biblical contexts and connotations of its use: [10]

1. It is used of the disciples *mending their nets* (Matthew 4:21). The idea is that the nets were being prepared for future use.
2. In Luke 6:40 it is said that a scholar cannot turn out better *equipped* than his teacher.
3. The word is used in Galatians 6:1 for *restoring* a brother who is taken in a fault.
4. There is a set of passages in which the word is

translated *to perfect or to complete what is lacking* (II Corinthians 13:11; I Thessalonians 3:10; Hebrews 13:21; I Peter 5:10).

5. In I Corinthians 1:10 it is translated "perfectly joined together" or drawing together the discordant elements in the church.

6. *The equipment of the saints* phrase found in Ephesians 4:12 may draw from a combination of these other images.

Do you know your spiritual gift(s), pastor? I am constantly amazed at the number of pastors and Christian workers I meet that do not know or are not sure. How can a pastor lead others to identify their gift(s) or model how a gift ought to be exercised in the body of Christ if he does not understand his own giftedness?

Each of us has a gift mix. Not all pastors will have the same gifts. For this reason, we will not be held accountable for the outcome of our ministries by the same standard as the next guy or the one after him and so on. We don't need to compare ourselves with others. We need to be content with the gifts we have received and remain humble concerning them—they are *gifts* after all—and we need to identify our gifts and minister within the framework that God designed and designated.

Corporately, the Lord adds to the church such as should be added. He adds the teachers we need, the helpers we need, the givers we need and the leaders we need. Grasp the overwhelming potential that neglecting spiritual gifts can destroy. There can be a literal breakdown of the ministry because people do not understand the role God has designed for them in His work in that place, which is your local church. The people needed for the ministries are before us each week. We have the resources. However, we do need to help those people to develop their gift mixes in order that together—yes, as a team—we may participate with God in a glorious and fruitful work that reaches our communities.

We can assert without argument that gifts and natural talents differ from one another and yet they can complement each other. However, we clearly understand that spiritual gifts are spiritual, an endowment from God to the believer at the moment of salvation for the purpose of edification of the body of Christ. As Paul describes it, we are gifted differently so that the whole body may be "fitly joined together."

Because spiritual gifts are the unique possession of believers, when a believer exercises his gift outside of the church building (in his community), he models a gift that the world cannot understand or possess apart from Christ. For example, a person with a gift for administration might offer to help a neighbor or family member balance his checkbook. A person with the gift of helps might help the boy living down the street fix the broken chain on his bike. The person with a gift of teaching may clean up the garage and open up a neighborhood reading room for children under school age. A person with the gift of mercy may visit a neighbor who has just broken his leg. The list of possibilities is endless.

Unbelievers ministered to in this way will become witnesses to something that is entirely supernatural, and over time many will ask, "From where do you receive this ability?" or "Why do you do these things you are doing?" The believer can then share Christ with that person who has already experienced the reality of the believer's testimony. This expanded application of spiritual gifts can ignite the evangelistic fervor in a congregation.

David asks a good question in Psalm 79:10: Why "should the heathen say, Where is their God?" They ask that because the church has often distanced itself from the world to such an extent that even when God does a marvelous thing in our midst, we are so far away from unbelievers that they do not have an opportunity to witness it.

Keep in mind the context of this discussion: I am not advocating compromise; we are not identifying with unbelievers; we are identifying with Christ among them. Spiritual gifts are not a part of our Christian experience; they are the outworking of that which God has worked in us, and although identifying and exercising them for the edification of the body is their primary purpose, they are much more than that. When we exercise spiritual gifts in this way, we love God AND love our neighbors as ourselves. An evangelistic use of spiritual gifts adds to the body, which multiplies the number and effectiveness of the team.

In the final analysis, we understand that God plants growing teams. Pastors and people, regardless of good intentions, cannot plan such a miracle of grace. However, we can avail ourselves of an intimate relationship with God that will produce a sensitivity in our hearts toward the work that God intends to do in our lives and in the lives of other believers He has planted in our ministries for the purpose of edification and teamwork. For these people we must constantly be thankful. Ministry is hard, but it is still a great privilege. And even though the challenges abound when we make the effort to build and work in teams, it is a great honor to work with and serve God's people. This need not be the season of our discontent.

I am concerned about the fact that Christianity has been lacking and is continuing to lack influence in our nation particularly and in this world. Moral decay abounds. However, the focus of today's ministry team should be directed towards reaching people one at a time with the gospel message. Leaders who believe in the cause of Christ must be willing to participate in the sacrifice and service of faith in this new millennium. It is necessary to grow. It is necessary to change. It is necessary to branch out like a banyan tree allowing Christ to extend our efforts beyond what we can see into the soil of the hearts of new disciples—building leadership teams that are rooted and grounded in Christ. It is imperative that we follow the Biblical pattern of team building and with one spirit and one mind strive together for the Faith of the Gospel.

CHAPTER 12

The Difference

"Men today know so much more than they do, with the result that they begin to question the things they know."[1]

Mingled among my memories of childhood are the words of preachers announcing that we were "living in the last days." The urgency of their message, especially when punctuated with warnings like "It could be tonight" or "I expect it within my lifetime," always stirred and, as a young boy, even scared me at times. But more often than not, it motivated me to live for Christ in the time given me, and it caused my heart to ache for those who were without Christ in this world. These men would open up the Scriptures and point to signs indicating a death of morality, a common European currency, an intensified anti-Semitism, etc.

Today, of course, these and many other Biblical prophecies are being fulfilled all around us. Amazingly, however, the church in America is less fervent, committed and involved than when I heard those messages years ago. Like Paul, I reason "that now it is high time to awake out of sleep: for now is our salvation nearer than when we believed."[2]

Christians in America today appear more concerned about creative religious entertainment than life-changing worship. Bible study and prayer times are mysteriously disappearing from our church calendars for lack of interest, and the average local church is merely marking time spiritually. Vance Havner once said, "The tragedy of today is that the situation is desperate, but the saints are not." With few exceptions most churches in America today are mirrored images of the Laodicean church spoken of in Revelation, chapter 3. In fact, many who began with hope and zeal have sadly adopted a "this is as good as it gets" attitude. They have been disillusioned and now act as if Laodiceanism is normal.

I believe it is time to pray—to yield to God who is not attracted to our strengths but to our weaknesses. It is time to admit, "Lord, without You we can do nothing; without You we can make no lasting difference in this new millennium." This, of course, cannot be accomplished without great effort and greater commitment.

I think that one point that has been well supported in this book is that ministry is anything but easy. However, I am convinced that God can and will use servant leaders who are both guided by and guiding by grace to make a difference in the immoral and, in some cases, heretical spiritual climate of our day, not unlike Daniel did in his own generation in Babylon. This, however, begs the questions: How can we effectively project God's light in this dark hour? How can we, as Christian leaders, truly make a difference?

Another church addressed in the Revelation was the one in Ephesus. Do you remember what the Lord had against them? They had lost their first love. Holy passion is being curiously replaced by fleshly excitement in many churches. There is a problem when our church services give the appearance of a pep rally. The Christian life can be both exciting and challenging, but these are not substitutes for passion—especially the passion of a first love. We are not called to *seriously like Christ*—we are called to a *love* relationship with Him.

Recently I was visiting with one of the men from our church who is a firefighter here in the Los Angeles area. I noticed that he seemed to be distracted and depressed. We spent some time together during which he shared with me that a few days prior he had been called to a residence where a young girl had fallen into a swimming pool. After pulling her out of the pool, he began administering CPR in an attempt to save her life. As he shared the story with me, he said, "Pastor, as I administered CPR, tears were rolling down my face as I realized that this young girl, not much older than my own daughter, was not responding."

I wonder if the Lord ever feels sorrow when He repeatedly seeks to revive His people, but there is no response. As I listened to the story and tried to encourage our church member, I uttered a prayer and asked the Lord to woo me again and again and again. I begged Him to create in me that desire that is like the deer panting for the water. I also prayed that I might sense the impending danger of judgment and separation from God that is the reality of so many lost with whom I come into contact daily.

Our Saviour could not look upon the crowds without being "moved with compassion," and yet many times those in Christian leadership are so consumed with organizational strategies and staff team tactics that even when they see people, they fail to see the reality of people without Christ. After time, we lose our first love; after time, we are unable to cry for or cry out to the lost. One believer has stated concern for evangelistic pitfalls in the form of a confession:

> *I'm sorry* that I only looked at what you were wearing instead of you. *I'm sorry* I assumed you wouldn't want me to talk to you so I never tried. *I'm sorry* that I shunned you when I should have offered a smile. *I'm sorry* that I passed by without

noticing you when I should have prayed. *I'm sorry*
I forgot that we are the same—the only difference
in my life is Christ. *I'm sorry* you only saw me
struggling instead of Him reaching out.[3]

Are we actually reaching the lost? Christian pollster
George Barna has reported in a number of surveys that
three-fourths of the church growth in our day is growth
from transfer of memberships from one church to
another. North American pastors need to be reminded
that the ministry is not about *paper* work—it is about *people* work. We must remain passionate toward God and His
purpose of reaching people with the Gospel. In II Corinthians 12:15, the Apostle Paul stated, "And I will very
gladly spend and be spent for you; though the more
abundantly I love you, the less I be loved."

Spiritual leadership requires passionate service. Great
leaders display courage in the ministry based on passion, not position, and you cannot have a passion for
the lost without a passion for the One whose passion
accomplished their salvation. Like Christ, and yet in our
own way and in our own day, we must be willing to "be
spent" for the salvation of others.

Notice that Paul stated, "Though the more abundantly I love you, the less I be loved." Human reasoning
rejects this reality of servant leadership as unfair. Doesn't
common sense tell us that the more we labor, the more
we ought to be loved and appreciated? However, we have
not been called to a fair game; rather, we have been
called as witnesses, martyrs who choose to die to self and
self's ambitions. Our hope is not in the love of others but
in Christ alone, the Hope of Glory. It is He who has
called us to serve Him passionately and has promised us
His unfailing love from which nothing and no one can
separate us. The leader whose constant concern is the
amount of appreciation he receives from people is without passion except possibly for himself. The leader

whose concern is to please Christ lovingly serves others until Christ reappears.

Often this passion is discovered in the prayer closet. That is one of the primary reasons why the church lacks passion: we don't pray, at least not as we should. I once heard a dear servant of the Lord, Dr. John R. Rice, say that "all of our failures are prayer failures." While it is God's place to intervene, it is our responsibility to inter-cede. If the church is going to make a difference in our generation, then we must begin to pray fervently. In fact, the mark of distinction among Christian believers in their personal lives and in their gatherings is the aroma of prayer. God can do more in the lives of His people during ten minutes of prayer than in ten minutes of preaching.

A dear Christian lady once told me that she had a hard time in church when pastors would preach about the Lord's return, especially when they would joyfully conclude, "I hope it is tonight!" Then many of them, she said, would smile big and laugh. She would visibly flinch when a preacher would say it and feel like crying when men "amen'd" it. She would think, *That's easy for them to say—all of their family members are saved; but what about the rest of the world?*

Although this woman was assured of her salvation and never doubted her own security in Christ, she had only been a believer for a couple of years. She struggled: *I bet they were saying that two years ago when I was with-out Christ and on my way to Hell. It's one thing to speak about the Lord's return, but why do they have to be so happy about it? Why do they laugh and smile? Why doesn't their heart break?*

As leaders we must pray for the lost with urgency, believing that our intercession invites God's interven-tion. Also, we must not fail to request the prayer of those with whom we serve in the ministry. The Apostle

Paul wrote, "Praying always with all prayer and supplication in the Spirit, and watching thereunto with all perseverance and supplication for all saints; And for me."[4]

> Prayer, then, is a duty expressly commanded for every Christian, all the time, and about everybody and everything. Not to pray is a sin, the sin of disobedience [with regard] to the plain and often repeated command of God. Lack of prayer is a sin. Doubtless, all of our sins, proud mistakes, and failures are prayer sins, prayer mistakes, and prayer failures.[5]

If we will see revival and the regeneration of many lost men and women, then it will begin with prayer to an almighty God whose intervention is the difference; for we have a living God whose delight is to answer prayer and to redeem those who are perishing.

What is the result of passion and prayer? I believe it is the effectual preaching of God's Word—a strong declaration of truth given forth through a vessel yielded to God. Servant leaders are mere vessels of clay in which God deposits His glory. Let us consider what it is "that always heralds the dawn of a reformation or revival. It is renewed preaching: not only a new interest in preaching, but a new kind of preaching. A revival of true preaching has always heralded [great] movements in the history of the church."[6]

I certainly support and practice *teaching* the Word of God, line upon line, precept upon precept. Teaching and one-on-one discipleship are vital parts of ministry, yet preaching has always been the engine that moves the local church.

It appears there has been a downplay of old-fashioned, declarative preaching which calls men and women back to God. Many churches market themselves as places where one will not have to "be preached at." This philosophy opposes the admonishment given in II Timothy

4:2 that instructs, "Preach the word; be instant in season, out of season; reprove, rebuke, exhort with all longsuffering and doctrine." In the next two verses Paul warns, "For the time will come when they will not endure sound doctrine; but after their own lusts shall they heap to themselves teachers, having itching ears; And they shall turn away their ears from the truth, and shall be turned unto fables."

We live in a day when religious teachers are scratching the itching ears of a generation that does not need to be coddled. Rather, people are literally dying, and that without Christ, to hear the Word of God rightly divided, preached in love and in truth with grace and authority that come from above—the Word that is able to convict and save the souls of men. If a preacher's strong declaration of truth bears censure or if he is labeled with some unfriendly term, then so be it. If he has delivered truth with grace and seasoned with salt, let that man rejoice in that he has fulfilled the commission of God and has not failed the One to whom he will give an account.

There will be no lasting difference made without Spirit-filled preaching. It pleases God to save people through "the foolishness of preaching." I can personally testify that the greatest spiritual decisions of my life, my "burning bush" experiences, have been prompted by God's Word preached unashamedly by men with a prayer life consistent with their passion. The preached Word creates a crisis of decision. It draws people to allow their beliefs about God to be determinative—that is, they will allow what they believe about God to affect how they live their daily lives.

Last Sunday morning at the close of a sermon I had preached, taking care to focus upon the Word, a dear couple came forward stating their desire to know the Lord Jesus Christ. I had sincerely thought that my *delivery* was ineffective—I wasn't "connecting." Then and now, I confess that it wasn't the message or my exegetical skill that drew this precious couple to the Lord. The power of the preached Word is indeed a mystery. However, I recognized that while I may not have made the difference, the considerable time I had spent in prayer and study that week had been the tool that God used to make an eternal difference in this couple's life.

America today needs a revival of old-fashioned, Spirit-led preaching that is well prepared both in the study and in the prayer closet. My hope is that as we have been entrusted with the message of salvation, so we will serve the Lord by leading men to Him through the declaration of His truth.

Section 6

Final Challenge

Final Challenge
Guided by Grace

The child who has only sailed his paper boat on the edge of a placid lake might wonder why enormous beams and bars of iron...are needed in making a ship. Ask the sailor, and he will answer. He says we must be prepared for something more than calm days. We must look ahead. The breakers will try us, the winds will put us to the test....We must be prepared for the worst as well as for the best.[1]

There are two basic kinds of leaders serving in ministry today. There are those who are *going through ministry* and those who are *growing through ministry.*

Growth cannot occur without change. However, change must be complemented by God's grace; otherwise, it is not godly change. Change for the sake of change is senseless. Change for the sake of conforming to another ministry is fleshly imitation. But change that results from the inner prompting of God's Spirit is an act of His grace on our behalf.

Frankly, if we are not changing, then probably we are not growing either. Of course this does not refer to abandoning Biblical doctrine and principles. The Apostle Paul warned the Thessalonian believers to avoid those who did not hold to the traditions or instructions that had been received.[2] If we are to grow into godly leadership, we must be willing to admit that there are areas of our lives that must change. And grace is God's "change agent" of truth. God's grace will never cause us to change in a way that violates His truth. "When God in grace deals with a man, He produces truth in a man,"[3] and there is no doubt that we who serve as leaders must walk in the steps of the One who was filled with grace and truth.

Sometimes God will use trials to lead us by His grace. At other times, He will change us through prayer or the preached Word. But ultimately it is His grace that is teaching us to deny sin and self and to live for His glory in this life.[4] The churches of this hour look for new and improved methods to reach the world. God seeks renewed and proven men, servant leaders, who will allow the God of all grace to teach, change and equip them, that they may lead others to the Source of all grace, which is Christ alone.

In short, if I will guide others into God's grace, *I must be guided by that same grace myself.* I must be **growing through ministry.** Yes, that means admitting mistakes, confessing sin, kneeling at an altar and perhaps getting back to some basics of the Christian life. God's grace creates an inner disposition to serve Him that is so compelling that the world and even many *comfortable* Christians will wonder at our faithfulness and joy in serving. And when they notice, or even when they don't, we will smile and know that His grace is real and that His grace is sufficient.

In Chapter 3, I shared about the Home-going of a special servant of God, Lori Thomason. I first met Lori several years ago in Tennessee when I interviewed her and her husband, Dave, for leadership positions on our staff. To our dismay, Lori was diagnosed with cancer. Her battle was valiant, and the spiritual growth of grace in her life convicted and confronted us with the privilege of knowing one woman whose sorrow and pain were transformed into beauty—the image of Christ.

A few weeks before Lori's passing, my wife, Terrie, visited her. Lori shared a prayer request. Her real regret in being bedridden, she confessed, was the fact that she could not serve in the ministries of the church. In her time of sorrow Lori was concerned for others.

She has reminded me of our Saviour who, while suffering on the cross, reminded John to care for His mother, Mary. He who was full of grace and truth was still concerned for others in His hour of need. Lori was a young woman who grew through her ministry of suffering.

Many pastors and Christian leaders are knowledgeable of the changes culturally, globally and technologically in these days. They quickly change worship styles, buy new computer systems and create new web pages. We are aware that the earth's population has doubled since 1951 and that the growth of Internet use is changing our world dramatically. We are working hard at organization and structural reengineering and at all things external. But are we truly growing in the grace of our Lord? Are we personally allowing God to prompt us, to grow us, to reengineer us?

Viktor Yazykov gained international fame when he operated on himself without anesthetic in the middle of the ocean. The 50-year-old Russian was 1,000 miles from shore in the South Atlantic when he realized that something was terribly wrong with his arm. Four days earlier he had joined a group of daring souls who set out from Charleston, South Carolina, on a 27,000-mile solo sailboat race around the world. This eight-month odyssey is called "Around Alone." Each competitor must navigate around the globe, and that's where things got sticky for Yazykov. His elbow, which had ached since leaving Charleston six weeks prior, was a double threat in that Yazykov needed both arms to survive at sea. Now the infection was posing a risk to his health. Without drastic measures he would certainly die before the closest boat could reach him. Using high-tech communication, Yazykov e-mailed Dr. Dan Carlin in Boston. Carlin runs a practice called World Clinic that provides emergency care through computer technology to people around the world. Carlin walked Yazykov through the 14-step surgical procedure via e-mail. With very deliberate instructions, Dr. Carlin told the seasoned sailor to "make your incision rapidly...it will hurt less if you do."

He also typed, "It hurts a great deal when you insert the gauze, but you must get it down into the depths of the wound as much as possible." The former Soviet commando tolerated the pain but became very concerned about his inability to stop the excessive bleeding. Before Dr. Carlin could respond back, Yazykov lost consciousness. Although e-mail was repeatedly sent throughout the night, no response came from the 40-foot *Wing of Change* sailboat. Twelve hours later, Yazykov typed in a simple message, "I AM OK." Within another five days he sailed into the port of Cape Town to the cheers of a crowd that had heard his story. After just three weeks' rest, Yazykov's arm was completely healed, and he set off on the second leg of the race to Auckland, New Zealand. By the middle of May 1999, Viktor Yazykov will sail into Charleston, South Carolina, after an incredible boat ride around the world. The success of this man's amazing journey is due in part to his willingness to experience great pain for the sake of healing. His self-inflicted incision lanced a deadly wound and opened up a passageway for healing.[5]

Do we need to forgive someone? His grace is sufficient! Is our desire to be equipped as a witness and minister of the Word in truth and in grace? His grace will empower and guide us. Do we need to develop a godly vision and purpose for ministry? His grace will lead us and illuminate our hearts.

One of my favorite hymns of consecration is "Where

He Leads Me I Will Follow." Perhaps you can recall the words to the first verse:

> I can hear my Saviour calling,
> I can hear my Saviour calling,
> I can hear my Saviour calling,
> "Take thy cross and follow, follow Me."

As we embark upon a new millennium of ministry, let us not forget the fourth verse of this treasured hymn, which encourages:

> He will give me grace and glory,
> He will give me grace and glory,
> He will give me grace and glory,
> And go with me, with me all the way.

I have sometimes felt God's Spirit lovingly but firmly calling me, "Make your incision rapidly; it will hurt less if you do." We should learn or awaken to the knowledge that God desires to glorify Himself in our lives and in our labors, leading us to conform to the beautiful image of His Son. His tool is grace; His method, change; and His promise reminds us that "the everlasting God, the LORD, the Creator of the ends of the earth, fainteth not, neither is weary...there is no searching of his understanding. He giveth power to the faint; and to them that have no might he increaseth strength....[and] they that wait upon the LORD shall renew their strength; they shall mount up with wings as eagles; they shall run, and not be weary; and they shall walk, and not faint."[6] The result is His glory.

My hope is that we will find our courage in His character and His strength in our weakness, mindful that "all things work together for good to them that love God, to them who are the called according to his purpose" (Rom. 8:28); and that in this faith we will discover that our own passage to growth in grace and glory is aboard the "Wings of Change"—change that is navigated by the Captain of our salvation, who also was made perfect through sufferings.[7]

Chapter Notes

Bible verses noted indicate an exact Scripture quotation, or they may be the source of those portions of Scripture that have been referred to or are paraphrased (paraphrase mine). All exact quotations of Scripture appear in the King James Version of the Bible.

It is not the wish of this author to endorse the ministry philosophy of any particular leader or author noted in this book.

Chapter 1
Enlisted in the Service of Grace

1. Crosby, Fanny J. Hymn—"Victory Through Grace," chorus.

2. II Timothy 3:16

3. Sanders, J. Oswald. *Spiritual Leadership*. Second Revision. Chicago, Illinois: Moody Press, 1967, p. 29.

4. Hebrews 13:9

5. I Corinthians 13:2

6. Small, D. H. *Design for Christian Marriage*. Westwood, New Jersey: Revell, 1959, p. 67.

7. Mark 10:29–31

8. Matthew 5:8

9. John 17:3

10. I John 3:23

11. Romans 12:8
12. I Peter 4:10

Chapter 2
Wanted: Servant Leaders

1. Maxwell, Mary E. Hymn—"Channels Only," verse 1.
2. Worden, Kirk (illustrator), *Discipleship Journal,* Issue 10, July 1, 1982. Volume 2, Number 4.
3. Hebrews 12:2
4. John 15:7
5. I Corinthians 11:1
6. Romans 3:23
7. Philippians 2:7–9
8. Psalm 119:57, 58
9. Matthew 20:25–28
10. I Corinthians 3:4
11. I Corinthians 4:1
12. I Corinthians 9:19, 22, 23

Chapter 3
A Model Who Works

1. John 13:4, 5
2. Galatians 4:19
3. II Timothy 4:16
4. I Corinthians 3:7–9
5. Bennett, Bill. *Thirty Minutes to Raise the Dead.* Cambridge, Ontario: Thomas Nelson Publishers, 1991, p. 95.
6. John 3:30
7. I Thessalonians 1:6
8. II Corinthians 8:1–5
9. I Thessalonians 5:13

10. Hemphill, Ken. *The Antioch Effect.* Nashville, Tennessee: Broadman & Holman Publishers, 1994, p. 83.

11. Ibid., p. 78.

Chapter 4
Go Forward

1. Berg, Lina Sandell. Hymn—"Day by Day," verse 1.

2. Proverbs 23:23

3. Isaiah 14:12–14

4. Veith, Gene Edward. *World* magazine. "Whatever Happened to Christian Publishing?" July 12–19, 1997. Volume 12, Number 12, p. 13.

5. Ibid.

6. McDowell, Josh. *How to Be a Hero to Your Kids.* Dallas, Texas: Word Publishing, 1991, p. 25.

7. Sanders, J. Oswald. *Spiritual Leadership.* Second Revision. Chicago, Illinois: Moody Press, 1967, p. 29.

8. I Thessalonians 2:3, 4

9. I Thessalonians 2:5–11

10. Ephesians 6:12, 13

11. Rice, John R. *Bible Giants Tested.* Murfreesboro, Tennessee: Sword of the Lord Publishers, 1962, p. 164.

12. II Timothy 2:3

13. Kennedy, John W. *Christianity Today,* "Jerry Falwell's Uncertain Legacy," December 9, 1996. Volume 40, Number 14, p. 63.

14. Ibid.

15. Barnett, Tommy. *There's a Miracle in Your House: God's Solution Starts With What You Have.* Orlando, Florida: Creation House Press, 1993, p. 84.

16. Stanley, Charles. *The Source of My Strength.* Nashville, Tennessee: Thomas Nelson Publishers, 1994, pp. 223+.

17. II Timothy 3:12
18. Proverbs 11:1

Chapter 5
Phoenix

1. Haugk, Kenneth G. *Antagonists in the Church.* Minneapolis, Minnesota: Augsburg Publishing House, 1988, p. 31.
2. Wiersbe, Warren. *Walking with the Giants.* Grand Rapids, Michigan: Baker Book House, 1971, p. 73.
3. Ibid.
4. Ibid., p. 263.
5. Ibid., p. 267.
6. Ibid.
7. II Timothy 2:24, 25
8. Psalm 119:71
9. Ibid.
10. John 1:14
11. II Timothy 3:12
12. II Corinthians 9:8
13. II Timothy 4:2
14. Ecclesiastes 3:1
15. Ecclesiastes 3:3–8
16. Titus 1:2
17. London, H. B., Jr., and Neil B. Wiseman. *Pastors at Risk.* Wheaton, Illinois: Victor Books, 1993, pp. 22 and 71.
18. Hurnard, Hannah. *Mountains of Spices.* Wheaton, Illinois: Tyndale House Publishers, 1977, p. 118.
19. Ibid., p. 121.
20. Psalm 35:1
21. I John 4:19

22. Smith, Shelton. Pamphlet: *When Unjust Critics Attack.* Murfreesboro, Tennessee: Sword of the Lord Publishers, 1997, p. 7.

23. James 4:6

24. II Corinthians 9:8

25. Ruth 1:16, 17

Chapter 6
Winds of Change

1. Anderson, Lynn. *They Smell Like Sheep.* West Monroe, Louisiana: Howard Publishing, 1997, p. 2.

2. Philippians 1:12

3. Psalm 27:7–9

4. Hurnard, Hannah. *Mountains of Spices.* Wheaton, Illinois: Tyndale House Publishers, 1977, p. 91.

5. Matthew 11:29

6. Dostoyevski, Fyodor. *The House of the Dead.* English translation by David McDuff. London, England: Penguin Books, p. 340.

7. Hebrews 11:4

8. Carmichael, Amy, arranged by David Hazard. *You Are My Hiding Place: Rekindling the Inner Fire (A devotional book).* Minneapolis, Minnesota: Bethany House Publishers, 1991, pp. 74+.

9. Hurnard, Hannah. *Mountains of Spices.* Wheaton, Illinois: Tyndale House Publishers, 1977, p. 70.

10. Luke 10:39

11. John 11:32

12. John 12:3

13. Acts 15:37–40; Colossians 4:10

14. II Timothy 4:9, 11

15. Luke 10:40–42

16. John 12:1–6; Mark 14:3–5
17. Jeremiah 32
18. Jeremiah 32:41
19. Jeremiah 32:27
20. Acts 20:28
21. I Corinthians 4:9
22. *Strong's Concordance,* "Greek Dictionary of the New Testament," Number 2302.
23. Philippians 1:6
24. Mark 12:28–31
25. II Corinthians 5:14–21
26. Hurnard, Hannah. *Mountains of Spices.* Wheaton, Illinois: Tyndale House Publishers, 1977, p. 95.
27. Ibid., p. 49.
28. II Samuel 12:1–13
29. II Samuel 16:5–13
30. Psalm 11:3

Chapter 7
Driver's Seat or Shotgun?

1. Titus 2:11, 12
2. Almy, Gary, with Carol Tharp Almy and Jerry Jenkins. *Addicted to Recovery.* Eugene, Oregon: Harvest House, 1994, p. 173.
3. Ibid., p. 178.
4. Ibid., p. 99.
5. James 1:22–24
6. Jude 4
7. Romans 6:5
8. Galatians 2:20
9. Ephesians 2:6

10. Romans 6:2, 11
11. Galatians 5:1–7

Chapter 8
Spirit-filled Semantics

1. Longstaff, William D. Hymn—"Take Time to Be Holy," verse 2.
2. Willmington, H. L. *Willmington's Guide to the Bible*. Wheaton, Illinois: Tyndale House Publishers, Inc., 1981, p. 589.
3. Jude 3
4. Hebrews 1:3
5. John 17:3
6. Barrett, David B., ed. *World Christian Encyclopedia*. New York, New York: Oxford University Press, 1982, p. 17.
7. Colossians 2:9
8. I Timothy 3:1–13; Titus 1:6–9 (paraphrase mine)
9. Riley, Pat. *The Winner Within*. Hudson, New York: G. P. Putnam's Sons, 1993, p. 58.
10. Acts 13:2
11. I Thessalonians 1:5, 6
12. I Peter 1:13–16
13. Morgan, G. Campbell. *The Crises of the Christ*. New York, New York: F. H. Revell Company, 1903, p. 109.

Chapter 9
Twilight Zone

1. Crosby, Fanny J. Hymn—"Rescue the Perishing," verse 3.
2. Proverbs 29:18
3. I Samuel 3:1
4. I Samuel 3:19
5. Joshua 1:3, 7–9

Chapter 10
Harvesting the Fruit

1. Wesley, Charles. Hymn—"A Charge to Keep I Have," verse 2.
2. Ephesians 4:11,12
3. II Timothy 2:2
4. Curtis, Gene. *The Measure of a Man.* Ventura, California: Regal Books, 1974, p. 36.
5. Ephesians 3:20
6. Philippians 1:27
7. II Corinthians 3:4–8,12,13
8. II Corinthians 3:17,18
9. Ortlund, Anne. *Discipling One Another: Discipline for Christian Community.* Dallas, Texas: Word Incorporated, 1979, p. 151.
10. Genesis 1:11
11. Acts 13:2
12. Colossians 1:3
13. Colossians 4:12,13
14. Matthew 11:29,30

Chapter 11
Banyan Trees and Building Teams

1. Kilmer, Joyce. *Trees and Other Poems.* New York, New York: George H. Doran Co., 1914, p. 18.
2. Allison et al., eds., "Something at the Root." This verse is from Richard Wilbur's poem "Seed Leaves," *The Norton Anthology of Poetry,* pp. 1201–1202 (out of print).
3. Proverbs 11:30
4. Hendricks, Howard G. *Teaching to Change Lives.* Portland, Oregon: Multnomah Press, 1987, pp. 121+.
5. Ibid., p. 123.

6. Hull, Bill. *The Disciple-Making Pastor.* Grand Rapids, Michigan: Fleming H. Revell, 1988, p. 197.

7. Finzel, Hans. *Top Ten Mistakes Leaders Make.* Wheaton, Illinois: Victor Books, 1994, p. 38.

8. Hendrix, John and Lloyd Householder, eds. *The Equipping of Disciples.* Nashville, Tennessee: Broadman Press, 1977, article by Brooks Faulkner, p. 25.

9. I Corinthians 12:18, 20–22

10. Hendrix, John and Lloyd Householder, eds. *The Equipping of Disciples.* Nashville, Tennessee: Broadman Press, 1977, article by Brooks Faulkner, pp. 25+.

Chapter 12
The Difference

1. Wiersbe, Warren, compiled by. *Classic Sermons on Christian Service* (sermon by G. Campbell Morgan). Grand Rapids, Michigan: Hendrickson Publishers, 1990, p. 33.

2. Romans 13:11

3. Melissa D. Baccarella

4. Ephesians 6:18, 19

5. Rice, John R. *Prayer—Asking and Receiving.* Murfreesboro, Tennessee: Sword of the Lord Publishers, 1942, p. 12.

6. Lloyd-Jones, Martyn D. *Preaching and Preachers.* Grand Rapids, Michigan: Zondervan Publishing House, 1971, pp. 24, 25.

Final Challenge
Guided by Grace

1. Wiersbe, Warren, compiled by. *Classic Sermons on the Attributes of God* (sermon by Joseph Parker—"God's Terribleness and Gentleness"). Grand Rapids, Michigan: Kregel Publications, 1989, p. 70.

2. II Thessalonians 3:1–6

3. Strombeck, J. F. *Grace & Truth.* Eugene, Oregon: Harvest House Publishers, 1982, p. 15.

4. Titus 2:11–13

5. Paraphrased from: O'Neill, Helen (Associated Press writer). Published in *The Houston Chronicle,* 1/3/99, p. 15A.

6. Isaiah 40:28–31

7. Hebrews 2:10

Reading List

The following books were not directly quoted; however, they have contributed to this author's ongoing
study of effective servant leadership.

Character Forged From Conflict
Gary D. Preston
Bethany House Publishers, 1999

Criswell's Guidebook for Pastors
W. A. Criswell
Broadman Press, 1980

Disciplines of Grace
R. Kent Hughes
Crossway Books, 1993

Failure: The Back Door to Success
Erwin W. Lutzer
Moody Press, 1975

For the Hurting Pastor
Ernest Pickering
Regular Baptist Press, 1987

Grace for Godly Living
From the pulpit ministry of Lancaster Baptist Church
Truth for Today Publications, 1997

He That Is Spiritual
Lewis Sperry Chafer
Zondervan Publishing House, 1918

Holy Burnout
Steve Roll
Virgil Hensley Publishing, 1996

Leading With Integrity
Fred Smith
Bethany House Publishers, 1999

Leading Your Church Through Conflict Reconciliation
Marshall Shelley, General Editor
Bethany House Publishers, 1997

Management Challenges for the 21st Century
Peter F. Drucker
Harper Business, 1999

Systematic Theology
Lewis Sperry Chafer
Dallas Seminary Press, 1947

The Bible Exposition Commentary
Warren Wiersbe
Victor Books, 1992, 1993, 1994

The Vance Havner Notebook
Vance Havner
Compiled by Dennis J. Hester
Baker Book House, 1989

For a complete list of books available from the Sword of the Lord, write to Sword of the Lord Publishers, P. O. Box 1099, Murfreesboro, Tennessee 37133.

(800) 251-4100
(615) 893-6700
FAX (615) 848-6943
www.swordofthelord.com